Endorsements

As a mother of two daughters, grandmother, great-grandmother, sister to eight women, a Christian woman, and a retired educator, I truly believe that this Teen Curriculum will be an excellent asset to the present and future young girls' lives.

—MRS. ESTELLE DAVIS

WOW! What an amazing resource for our girls and young ladies discussing relevant topics, like self-esteem, friendships, faith, and individuality. Prevailing world views are confronted through the lens of the Lord Jesus Christ. I gladly recommend this Teen Curriculum for girls and wish I had access to this when my daughter was a young teenager.

—MR. DAMON ROSS

I truly believe it is so important to provide young girls with encouragement and know their identity is not of the world but in Christ alone. I believe that a girl's guide for surviving the teen years will provide and give the tools young girls need to conquer and face the challenges of life.

—MS. ISABELLA ROSS

The Teen Curriculum for girls is an in-depth 24-week program to teach self-esteem, self-love, and peer-pressure issues. These values are taught through biblical lessons, contemporary music, and question/answer time with the instructor and peers. I strongly believe that this program is valuable and much needed for all tween and teenage girls.

—MR. CREIG MILLER

YOU Are A Masterpiece

A TEEN EMPOWERMENT GUIDE

Sheila L. Ross

You Are a Masterpiece
A Teen Empowerment Guide

Unless otherwise noted, scripture quotations are taken from the English Standard Version (ESV), King James Version (KJV), and New King James Version (NKJV) of the Bible.

ISBN: 979-8-35091-582-2
ISBN eBook: 979-8-3509-1583-9

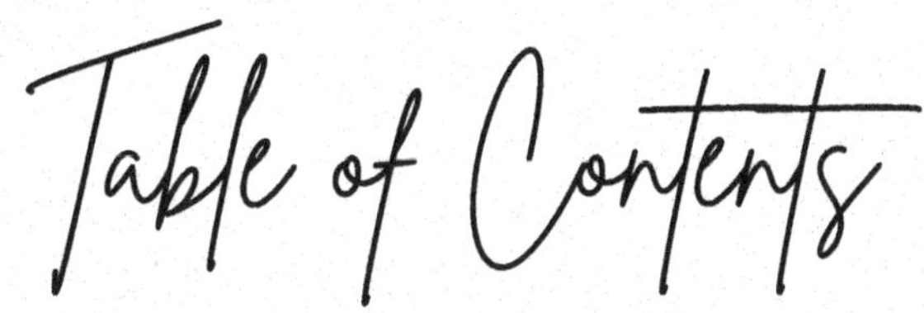

Introduction 1

Purpose 3

Acknowledgements 5

About the Author 7

Curriculum Structure 9

Discussion Topics and Activities 11

Teacher Lessons Week 1-24 15

Weekly Class Evaluation 103

Attachments 105

Appendix A: Key Terms 107

Teen Curriculum 113

Student Copy Supplemental Resource 163

References 173

Positive Affirmations 175

Positive Character Traits 177

Youtube Videos 179

Weekly Lessons

Week 1: Self-Esteem

Week 2: Self-Worth

Week 3: Self-Acceptance

Week 4: Self-Love

Week 5: Self-Respect

Week 6: Self-Integrity

Week 7: Friendships

Week 8: Individuality

Week 9: Influence

Week 10: Depression

Week 11: Exercise

Week 12: Attitude

Week 13: Insecurity

Week 14: Responsibility

Week 15: Fear

Week 16: Faith

Week 17: Love

Week 18: Music

Week 19: Prayer

Week 20: Obedience

Week 21: Peace

Week 22: Behavior

Week 23: Peer Pressure

Week 24: Stress

Introduction

MY NEPHEW DAMON has been very instrumental before and during the writing process of *You Are A Masterpiece.* He has always encouraged me by telling me for years, "Aunt Sheila, you need to write a book so that others can benefit from the talents, gifts, creativity, and wisdom that God has given you."

One of the reasons why I began this journey of writing for teens was because of the love and passion that I have for them to survive, thrive, and overcome life's challenges. The middle-school students whom I taught and mentored were attempting to solve every-day adolescent concerns regarding how to manage school, home life, friendships, dating, and peer pressures by using social media for guidance as the final authority. After using the advice of popular people, whom they did not know and continuing to fall short in relationships the students would come to me seeking guidance.

Purpose

MY PURPOSE FOR WRITING this Christian Teen Curriculum was to equip and empower young girls with the necessary resources to establish and maintain a positive self-image by using God's Word as the foundation for a purposeful and successful life. The Christian Teen Curriculum teaching will not only increase a girl's self-esteem, self-worth, and self-image but will also assist her in making better choices in life. Then, the girls who have benefited from the teaching of the self-love will be able to influence and teach other girls how to value and love themselves according to godly standards. This will create a new culture for young girls for generations to come who will feel empowered, be proud of their bodies, accept their uniqueness and know their value and worth. They will not have to look to society to define their existence and will know that they were fearfully and wonderfully created by God.

"Our daughters might be smart and kind, and they might be great businesswomen, wonderful mothers, but unless they understand their purpose in life and see it as something bigger than themselves, they will not internally be happy." (Dr. Meg Meeker, p. 125). It begins with teaching them that this world does not evolve only around them, but it is about serving God. God is the one who made us and the one who has a plan for our lives. According to Dr. Meeker, our daughters will always be restless, unsatisfied, and unfulfilled until she finds faith in God which is the truth for her mere existence.

The Teen Curriculum will assist the girls in unlearning the ungodly, trendy societal standards and have them relearn and renew their mind by applying God's standards and holding themselves accountable according to what the bible says about their value and worth.

They will understand that they do not have to compromise their morale's, compare themselves with other girls or get their identity from social media experts. They will learn how to be the best version of themselves because there is no one else like them in the world. They are truly unique and a beautiful masterpiece.

The Teen Curriculum focuses on providing young girls with a solid Christian foundation in discovering who they are according to the Word of God by meditating and applying the scripture references to everyday situations. Here is a list of topics that will be discussed along with scripture references: self-esteem, self-worth, self-acceptance, self-love, self-respect, self-integrity, making and maintaining friendships, individuality, influence, depression, exercise, attitude, insecurity, responsibility, fear, faith, love, music, prayer, obedience, and peace.

The Teen Curriculum will also teach the girls how to survive life's overwhelming external and internal factors such as coping with school and home pressures, hormonal changes, puberty, and social woes. Often, the girls do not know where to turn, so they turn to social media, TV, or friends for advice and guidance. During this age, a girl's feelings are validated by someone who loves them. As adults, we need to be very cautious whenever we approach them as they go through growth issues and concerns.

Some of the problems and issues that they face will usually affect their relationships with family and friends and interfere with their schoolwork, extra-curricular activities, sleep, and self-image.

Also, the Teen Curriculum will afford them the opportunity to help identify their personal struggles ahead of time and provide them with solutions on how to solve them. It will also open the door for heart-to-heart conversations that will provide a platform for the girls to discuss their problems and feelings with a trusted friend or an adult. Their testimony will be a witness to others on how the Word of God can transform hearts, minds and renew thinking.

As adults, when trying to assist the girls with daily pressures, we must come from a place of humility, empathy, vulnerability, and transparency so that the girls do not feel odd, weird, or alone. If we do not accept and meet the girls where they are at this delicate stage in life, we will miss an opportunity to influence and make an impact on their lives. And unfortunately, we may even lose them, and they will seek attention, love, and acceptance from all the wrong people and places in trying to fit into the world. "Nobody's life is free from adversity and that's okay. You can't protect your children from hardship nor is it your job to keep them from ever feeling pain, disappointments, or struggle." (Dr. Charles Soply, p.165). Dr. Soply goes on to say that it is the parent's job to set their children up to be able to respond with strength and resilience. Parents should give their child an opportunity to at least try even if they might struggle.

This Curriculum for girls which will help equip and empower young girls to recognize their value, self- worth and help them to establish a positive self-image which includes boundaries, standards, principles, and morals according to biblical standards.

This curriculum will help girls recognize their God-given talents, gifts, and purpose in life. I want the girls to see themselves as a unique masterpiece, fearfully and wonderfully made by the creator, who continues to mold and shape them into the person that can be used by Him for His Kingdom work. God sees us not as where we are but our destination in life and He is shaping us each day to become more like His son, Jesus Christ. To God be the glory. Amen.

Acknowledgements

I WOULD LIKE TO THANK the following people for their support in editing and reviewing this Curriculum: Joyce Kerlegon, Olga Miller, and Karen Irizarry. I also would like to thank my family, friends and Michael who continued to pray, motivate and encourage me along this blessed journey.

This Curriculum is dedicated to my parents, Earl Edward Sr. and Mary Lee Ross, to whom I owe so much. They loved me unconditionally, introduced me to the Lord at an early age, took me to Sunday school and church, and instilled in me so many Christian values, morals, and spiritual principles; for that I am ever grateful.

About the Author

MS. ROSS received a foundation for her love of God's Word from Citizens of Zion Missionary Baptist Church, pastored by Dr. Bobby T. Newman Sr. and Charmaine Newman. She continued growing in the word of God under the teachings of Pastors Bayless and Janet Conley at Cottonwood Church.

Ms. Ross began teaching third-grade students at Bethany Christian Academy elementary and middle school for five years. This was where she acquired a love for working with students who had learning disabilities. She left Bethany and then worked at Norwalk La-Mirada Unified School District for twenty years where she taught middle- and high-school students in a mild to moderate special education setting for eighteen years.

For two years, Ms. Ross worked as a teacher on Special Assignment at the Norwalk La-Mirada Unified School District, developing and modifying curriculums for special education students along with instructing the teachers on how to implement it. Ms. Ross has attended and completed numerous educational workshops and seminars for personal and educational development.

Curriculum Structure

THE CURRICULUM can be taught in diverse settings such as, workshops, small group, mentor programs, church, Sunday school, after-school programs, workshops, behavioral programs, positive reinforcement programs, schools, and home school settings.

The structure of the Curriculum has been designed to be user-friendly. It is a complete program with twenty-four subject matters that concern parents and our youth. Located in the program, you will find lessons which include an agenda, Bible scriptures, key terms, discussion questions, and everyday scenarios.

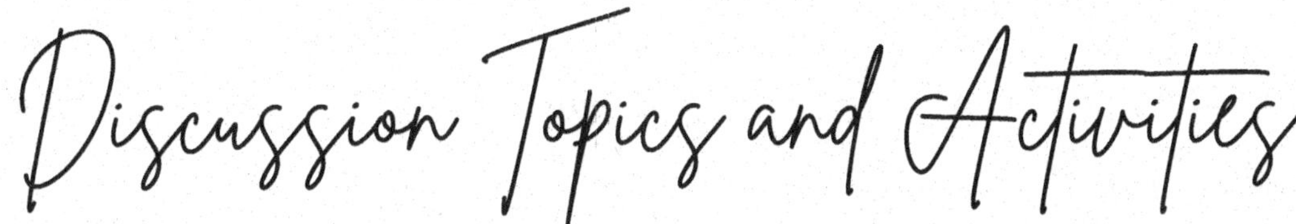

Discussion Topics and Activities

- Week 1: Self-Esteem and Body Image ("Flaws" Song Video by Kierra Sheard)
- Week 2: Self-Worth ("I Am Not My Hair" Song Video by India Arie) ("Jireh" Elevation Worship)
- Week 3: Self-Acceptance ("Video" Song Video by India Arie)
- Week 4: Self-Love ("The Greatest Love" Song Video by Whitney Houston/Celine Dion)
- Week 5: Self-Respect: An Acrostic Poem for the Word "Self-Respect" or Your Name
- Week 6: Self-Integrity ("The Champion" Song Video by Carrie Underwood/Ludacris)
- Week 7: Friendship(s) ("See You Again" Song Video by Wiz Khalifa/Charlie Puth)
- Week 8: Individuality ("Don't You Worry 'Bout a Thing" Song Video by Kelly Tori)
- Week 9: Influence: Write a Summary of Who Has Influenced You in Life
- Week 10: Depression ("Lovely Day" Song Video by Demi Lovato)
- Week 11: Exercise
- Week 12: Attitude ("Happy" Song Video by Pharrell)
- Week 13: Insecurity ("Roar" Song Video by Katie Perry)
- Week 14: Responsibility
- Week 15: Fear ("No Fear" Song Video by Kari Jobe)
- Week 16: Faith ("Always Win" Song Video by Kierra Sheard)
- Week 17: Love ("Spread Love" Song Video by Take Six)
- Week 18: Music ("I'll Find You" Song Video by Lecrae/Tori Kelly)

- Week 19: Prayer ("The Prayer" Song Video by Andrea Bocelli/Celine Dion)
- Week 20: Obedience
- Week 21: Peace ("Imagine" Song Video by John Lennon)
- Week 22: Behavior/Conduct
- Week 23: Peer Pressure (Role Playing-Skits)
- Week 24: Stress ("Under-Pressure Mindfulness for Teens" at www.2bpresent.com)

Weekly Class Activities Agenda

(RECOMMENDED TIME: 1 HOUR):

- Attendance (2 minutes)
- Ice Breakers/Good News/Sharing/Praise Reports (2 minutes)
- Beginning Prayer (1 minute)
- Discuss/Virtual and/or Classroom Norms (2 minutes) (Examples in Attachments)
- Song Video ("Flaws" with lyrics by Kierra Sheard) (Video Time 3:16)
- Discussion Topic Question(s) (25 minutes)
- Plan of Salvation (As needed 2–5 minutes)
- Ending Prayer (2 minutes)
- Class Evaluation (Google Form) (7 minutes) Q&A
- Affirmations (3 minutes) (Students provide positive words to others)
- Prayer Cards (Filled out by the students for personal prayers) (5 minutes)
- Self-Reflection Cards (Filled out by the students) (5 minutes)

(THIS SECTION MAY NOT BE REPRODUCED)

How to Teach?

The teacher will follow the Weekly Class Activities Agenda and structure of each lesson.

Beginning Prayer (Sample)

Dear God bless this day that you have made and help us to rejoice and be glad in it. Give us clarity of mind, revelation of who you are, wisdom, knowledge, and discernment on how to apply each lesson to our life. Guide and direct our footsteps and show us your will and purpose for our life. Thank you for blessing us so that we may be a blessing to others. In Jesus name, Amen.

Purpose: This lesson aims to increase the girls' self-esteem by reminding them that they are fearfully and wonderfully made by God and are created in His image.

Key Terms: discernment, entourage, stature false metric narrative, adorn, apparel and, renewing.

Week 1

Self-Esteem, Body Image, and Dress Code

Self-esteem is a person's belief about their worth and value. Our self-esteem is important because it influences our choices and decisions. "Teenagers feel good about themselves for well-earned accomplishments and meaningful contributions." (Dr. Lisa Damour, p. 67)

Select the best example that pertains to low self-esteem:

1. Susan is always the last girl to be picked for any type of sports in physical education class because she is not athletic and very timid. Susan is very intelligent and a caring person but has been very distant from the other students since the family's recent homeless situation. Karen, the volleyball team captain, yells out loud in front of the entire class, "Susan, please get away from me; you smell like a dirty bum." Susan, becomes embarrassed and runs off the volleyball court in tears. Janessa runs after Susan to make sure she is okay.
2. Jennifer is walking to school alone when a classmate in a black car yells out the window, "Hey, lovely Jenny." Jenny ignores the classmate in the black car and continues walking to school without batting an eye.

Answer: 2

Discussion Topic Questions:

Why is having self-esteem important?

How do we acquire self-esteem?

Instruction: Provide thirty seconds of wait time for the girls to respond to the question. If no one answers, then the panel and/or the coordinator will respond to the question.

Answer:

My self-esteem and/or value is in who God says I am. I can find it in the Word of God, which is the Bible. We need to reject a false world metric or narrative of a girl's worth and value. Get to know you and spend some time with you. By doing this, it will allow you to see yourself through a pair of healthy eyes.

Ask God to give you wisdom and discernment on who you allow in your inner circle to speak in your life. Know that you are enough by yourself and do not need an abundance of friends, or an entourage. You are unique, just like a snowflake, and you do not need to copy or wear someone else's brand. God only made one of you so that you do not have to compare yourself with another person. The only pressure that you should have is for competing with the best version of yourself. What are you passionate about in life? What have you dreamt of doing in life? Learn to master you and who God has called you to be. Experience real commitment in God and what He has purposed for you in life. "What people we look to for affirmation of our worth treat us as though we are expendable to them. It crushes our soul and fractures our identity."1 (Nona Jones, p.81). " The most difficult work we have to do is in ourselves1(Nona Jones, p.36)

Dr. Damour also stated in her book, "Emotional Lives of Teenagers", that pre-teens and teens find a sense of self-esteem when they accomplish a goal in an activity. Some of their interests may include doing a flip on a trampoline, drawing or painting, try skateboarding, baking a cake, cooking a dish for dinner, starting a blog, bowling, reading a book, jewelry making, create a YouTube Video, indoor skydiving. Teens like exploring things that have no grade attached to it.

Play Youtube.com Video ("Flaws" by Kierra Sheard, 3 minutes 16 seconds)

What does the Bible say about "self-esteem," "body image," and "dress code"?

Scriptures:

A. You are Fearfully and Wonderfully Made (Psalms 139:13–14) (ESV)

B. You are altogether beautiful, my love; there is no flaw in you. (Song of Solomon 4:7) (ESV)

C. But the Lord said to Samuel, do not look on his appearance or the height of his stature because I have rejected him. For the Lord sees not as man sees; man looks on the outward appearance, but the Lord looks on the heart. (1 Samuel 16:7) (ESV)

D. Do not be transformed into this world but by the renewing of your mind. (Romans 12:2) (ESV)

E. But ye are a chosen generation, a royal priesthood, a holy nation, a peculiar people: that ye should shew forth the praises of Him who has called you out of darkness into His marvelous light. (1 Peter 2:9) (KJV)

Dress Code: Dress code is a style of dress that a person has adopted to express who they are from the outside.

Discussion Questions: How do you decide what clothing to wear in public or to school? What is acceptable and appropriate clothing for your age?

Answer:

We decide what to wear depending on the event or activity. The Word of God also informs us on how we should adorn ourselves. "Every woman must know that looks and "curves" will fade away. Your character is for life."2 (R.C. Blakes Jr., p.109)

"Why are we letting men tell us how to dress when at the beginning of their life, mom is telling them how to dress." Their wives or girlfriends are dressing them too. Create your name brand and dress code that fits who you are. R.C. Blakes Jr. also stresses that a girl or woman should let her dress code be consistent with her moral code.

Scriptures:

A. Likewise, also that women should adorn themselves in respectable apparel, with modesty and self-control, not with braided hair and gold or pearls or costly attire. (1 Timothy 2:9) (ESV)

B. Or do you not know that your body is a temple of the Holy Spirit within you, whom you have from God. (1 Corinthians 6:19–20) (ESV)

Ending Prayer/Prayer of Salvation:

Dear Jesus, please forgive me for all my sins. I believe you died on the Cross and rose again. Come into my life and help me trust and follow you. I accept you as Lord and Savior over my life; in Jesus's name, Amen.

Weekly Class Activities Agenda

(RECOMMENDED TIME: 1 HOUR):

- Attendance (2 minutes)
- Good News (2 minutes)
- Beginning Prayer (1 minute)
- Discuss Virtual Class Norms (2 minutes)
- Song Video ("I Am Not My Hair" by India Arie) (Video Time 3:44)
- Discussion Topic Questions (25 minutes)
- Plan of Salvation (2–5 minutes)
- Ending Prayer (2 minutes)
- Class Evaluation (Google Form) (7 minutes) Q&A
- Affirmations (3 minutes)
- Prayer Cards (5 minutes)
- Self-Reflection (5 minutes)

How to Teach?

The teacher will follow the Weekly Class Activities Agenda.

Beginning Prayer

Dear God bless this day that you have made and help us to rejoice and be glad in it. Give us clarity of mind, revelation of who you are, wisdom, knowledge, and discernment on how to apply each lesson to our life. Guide and direct our footsteps and show us your will and purpose for our life. Thank you for blessing us so that we may be a blessing to others. In Jesus name, Amen.

Purpose: This lesson aims to teach and discuss why it is crucial to develop a positive self-worth.

Key Terms: sinners, inward

Week 2

Self-Worth/Emotions/Feelings

Self-worth is how you value yourself. You are a good person and would like to be treated with self-respect. "Know your value, set standards, and don't compromise for anyone." (Tony and Sheri Gaskins, p.21)

Select the best example that pertains to knowing your self-worth:

1. Karen is getting ready for school and is putting on her mandated school uniform that consists of a navy-blue cotton skirt and a maroon polo shirt with the school's name embroidered on the front. Karen's friends tease her for dressing like a nerd. Karen informs them that she likes looking studious at school because it makes her feel and learn like a student. She saves her other clothes for the weekends.
2. Clementine is dressing up for the Picture Day today at the middle school. She decides to wear cut-off jeans and a thin red-striped midriff top to show off the body piercing above her navel area. She got the body piercing because Jeremy told her it would make her look good.

Answer: 1

Discussion Topic Question: How do you measure or determine your self-worth?

Instruction: Provide thirty seconds of wait time for the girls to respond. If no one answers, then the panel and/or coordinator will respond to the question.

Answer:

Self-worth is not determined by what you have or what others think about you. It comes from within. External forces do not define it. Too often, we have noticed how our sense of self-worth affects us, but we rarely take the time to see how we calculate self-worth. Is it determined by the kind of life that we live? Do we allow other people to determine our self-worth? When you know who you are and are happy with the person you have become, you will experience a sense of self-worth and peace through life's struggles or ups and downs. God will give you that sense of peace that surpasses all understanding.

Our self-worth is not found in us, but it comes from Christ who chose us before the foundation of the world, that we should be holy and blameless before Him, in love He predestined us. (Ephesians 1:4) (ESV). He established the foundations of the world (Genesis 1:26–27) (ESV). We were created in His image (Psalms 139:14) (ESV). We have been fearfully and wonderfully made. Wonderful are your work.

So, how much does God value us? Jesus Christ died for us while we were yet sinners (Romans 5:8) (ESV). The fact that Jesus Christ died on the Cross for our sins gives us a good indication of how valuable we are to God.

I have heard Joseph Prince say, "So, it's time to stop allowing your weaknesses and shortcomings to deceive you into feeling trapped and held back from living the good life God has for you. It's time to stop making excuses to throw in the towel, telling yourself, 'Things will never change for me.' Friend, nothing could be further from the truth because you have the grace of God on your side!"

God's thoughts are always on us, they are too many for me to count; they outnumber the grains of sand on earth (Psalms 139:17–18) (ESV). Creating our self-worth after God has given it to us is inherently prideful because it implies that we think we can do a better job at it than God, or that what He has given us is not enough. The best way that we can measure our self-worth is to focus on how He sees us. We should not allow the world to define our self-worth because their way of measuring self-worth is different from God's way. For the Lord sees not as the world sees: the world looks on the external appearance, but the Lord looks at the heart (1 Samuel 17:7) (ESV).

"My advice to younger sisters may make you smile says R.C. Blakes Jr..

"Don't work on increasing your bust line. Work on increasing your bottom line through education and personal initiative." (R.C. Blakes Jr, p.54)

Play Youtube.com Video, ("I Am Not My Hair" by India Arie, 3 minutes 44 seconds)

What does the Bible say about "self-worth?"

Scriptures:

A. For you formed my inward parts: you knitted me together in my mother's womb (Psalms 139:13–14) (ESV)

B. But God shows his love for us in that while we were still sinners, Christ died for us. (Romans 5:8) (ESV)

C. How precious also are thy thoughts unto me, O God: How great is the sum of them! If I should count them, they are more in number than the sand. When I awake I am still with thee. (Psalms 139:17–18) (KJV)

D. For I know the thoughts that I think towards you, saith the Lord, thoughts of peace, and not of evil, to give you an expected end. (Jeremiah 29:11) (KJV)

E. And we know that all things work together for good to them that love God, to them who are called according to His purpose. (Romans 8:28) (KJV)

Ending Prayer/Prayer of Salvation:

Prayer of Salvation:

Dear Jesus, please forgive me for all my sins. I believe you died on the Cross and rose again. Come into my life and help me trust and follow you. I accept you as Lord and Savior over my life; in Jesus's name, Amen.

Weekly Class Activities Agenda

(RECOMMENDED TIME: 1 HOUR)

- Attendance (2 minutes)
- Good News (2 minutes)
- Beginning Prayer (1 minute)
- Discuss Virtual Class Norms (2 minutes)
- Panel Introduction (2 minutes)
- Song Video ("Video" by India Arie) (Video Time 2:23)
- Discussion Topic Question(s) (20 minutes) Q&A
- Plan of Salvation (2–5 minutes)
- Ending Prayer (2 minutes)
- Class Evaluation (Google Form) (5 minutes)
- Affirmations (3 minutes)
- Prayer Cards (5 minutes)
- Activity (3 minutes)
- Self-Reflection (5 minutes)

How to Teach?

The instructor will follow the Weekly Class Activities Agenda.

Beginning Prayer

Dear God bless this day that you have made and help us to rejoice and be glad in it. Give us clarity of mind, revelation of who you are, wisdom, knowledge, and discernment on how to apply each lesson to our life. Guide and direct our footsteps and show us your will and purpose for our life. Thank you for blessing us so that we may be a blessing to others. In Jesus name, Amen.

Purpose: This lesson aims to help girls accept their good qualities, flaws, and failures.

Key Terms: faith, grace

Week 3

Self-Acceptance

Self-acceptance is the acceptance of one's strengths and weaknesses. What do I like/What don't I like? I have a history of living my life too concerned with how other people viewed me. I cared so much about what other people thought of me that I never took time to assess my own thoughts." (Sarah Jakes Roberts, p.39). "Whatever their benefits for some girls, many girls find that social media platforms create havoc and pain in their lives." (Dr. Meg Meeker, p. 26) She continues to shed light on that parents should tell their daughters that if they are striving for social media popularity it is not real popularity. Social media posts and tweets are considered being very shallow. While they are paying attention to social media they are missing out on living and experiencing real not virtual world. I cared so much about what other people thought of me that I never took time to assess my own thoughts." (Sarah Jakes Roberts, p.39).

Select the best answer that shows how you accept weaknesses:

1. On the math exam, Josephine received a 54 percent, and Tanya got an 86 percent. Tanya was bragging and boasting about her score and called Josephine "stupid." Josephine responded by saying, "I will start going to math tutoring with the teacher after school because I struggle with basic algebra concepts and algebraic expressions this school year.
2. Ronnie scored a 62 percent n the math exam, and Beyonce scored a 96 percent. Ronnie told Chris that she failed the math exam because Mr. Stafford, the math teacher, does not like her and must fail someone to keep his job.

Answer: 1

Discussion Topic Questions: Who am I?

I am a child of God, and I was bought with a price.

What self-talk are you doing to encourage yourself?

Instruction: Provide thirty seconds of wait time for the girls to respond to the question. If no one answers, then the panel and/or coordinator will respond to the question.

Answer:

I am a good and caring person, and I deserve to be treated with the same respect that I give a person. I am loved. I am allowed to make mistakes and learn from them. I am forgiven and taught by Jesus Christ's example on how to forgive others.

What do I like about myself?

I like that that I am unique. I am alive. I am intelligent. I am courageous. I am a great friend. I am fearfully and wonderfully made.

Can you look in the mirror and truly accept how unique you are? You are a work in progress. God is not done with you yet. Do you welcome your flaws along with your failures? As I think about who I am, I realize that some of the belief systems that I have about myself came from others who were supposed to love and encourage me but did not. The self-hatred also came from an image of what society and social media suggested I should look like. My self-judgments were based on what others said about me. They were also formed by what my parents saw. "The answer of course is that owning your voice is a super-power that every girl needs to succeed. The ability to turn inward confidence into action by speaking out is one of the most crucial life skills your daughter will rely on, as a young adult and for years to come." (Dr. Marisa Porges, p.29) Dr. Porges continues to stress that nurturing a girl's ability to effectively speak up for herself is very critical in helping her to be independent emotionally and intellectually. Helping your child to navigate the ups and downs in life gives her self-acceptance and confidence. This will help at school, in relationships, with teachers and friends. It will also allow her to find her voice and be able to self-advocate which is very important skill needed in life. The higher that you climb in life people need to see that you have a voice and feel comfortable with who you are. When people believe in you, they will follow you. It produces excellent leadership skills.

Play Youtube.com Video ("Video" by India Arie, 2 minutes 23 seconds)

What does the Bible say about "self-acceptance?"

Scriptures:

A. For by grace, you have been saved through faith. And this is not your own doing. (Ephesians 2:8) (ESV) (Psalms 139: 13–14) (ESV)

B. For you created my inmost being you knit me together in my mother's womb. I praise you because I am fearfully and wonderfully made; your works are wonderful. I know that full well. (Psalms 139:13-14) (NIV)

C. Being confident of this, that He who began a good work in you will carry it on to completion until the day of Christ Jesus. Philippians 1:6) (NIV)

Activities: (You will need an electronic device or paper)

List five of your positive qualities on a sheet of paper.

List three things that you wish you could change about yourself.

List what you learned about yourself when you were young, from those close to you, such as mother, father, siblings, teachers, classmates, etc. What message do you focus on today? What do you believe about yourself, and what beliefs detract from your confidence and happiness? Are these messages or opinions accurate or something that you think are true? Which statements do you want to change that will help your self-esteem? What new thoughts would help support your beliefs and help keep your self-esteem?

Ending Prayer/Prayer of Salvation:

Prayer of Salvation:

Dear Jesus, please forgive me for all my sins. I believe you died on the Cross and rose again. Come into my life and help me trust and follow you. I accept you as Lord and Savior over my life; in Jesus's name, Amen.

Weekly Class Activities Agenda

(RECOMMENDED TIME: 1 HOUR):

- Attendance (2 minutes)
- Good News (2 minutes)
- Beginning Prayer (2 minutes)
- Discuss Virtual Class Norms (2 minutes)
- Panel Introduction (2 minutes)
- Song Video ("The Greatest Love of All" by Whitney Houston/Celine Dion) (Video Time 5:22)
- Discussion Topic Question(s) (16 minutes)
- Class Discussion Question(s) or Self-Reflection Question (email) (10 minutes)
- Plan of Salvation (5 minutes)
- Ending Prayer (2 minutes)
- Class Evaluation (Google Form) (7 minutes)
- Affirmations (3 minutes)

How to Teach?

The teacher will follow the Weekly Class Activities Agenda.

Beginning Prayer

Dear God bless this day that you have made and help us to rejoice and be glad in it. Give us clarity of mind, revelation of who you are, wisdom, knowledge, and discernment on how to apply each lesson to our life. Guide and direct our footsteps and show us your will and purpose for our life. Thank you for blessing us so that we may be a blessing to others. In Jesus name, Amen.

Purpose: This lesson aims to teach girls how to love themselves first and love others.

Key Terms: nourishes, cherishes, and workmanship.

Week 4

Self-Love

Self-love is loving yourself and taking care of your needs and happiness.

Select the best answer that pertains to taking the time to love yourself first:

1. Mary is in the lunch line with some of her friends. Jane asks Mary for $3.50 to purchase lunch. Mary only has $4.50 for lunch, and she gives Jane $3.50 because Jane says that she will pay her back tomorrow. Mary uses the remaining $1.00 to purchase a bag of hot Cheetos with lime for her lunch.
2. Christina forgot her lunch money today and asked Joanna if she could borrow $3.50 until tomorrow. Joanna informed Christina that she only had enough money to purchase lunch for herself and that she was famished after running the mile for the physical education class today. Joanna told Christina that she could go to the front office and call home for someone to bring her the lunch money.

Answer: 2

Discussion Topic Questions: What is self-love?

Instruction: Provide thirty seconds of wait time for the girls to respond to the question. If no one answers, then the panel and/or coordinator will respond to the question.

Answer:

Self-love means that you accept everything about yourself. Self-love is the foundation that allows you to have confidence, maintain healthy relationships, set boundaries, set goals for yourself, practice self-care, and feel proud of who you are.

Discussion Topic Question: Why is it important to love yourself? List four reasons.

Answer:

1. It is essential to love yourself because God made you out of love, and He does not make any mistakes.
2. Self-love not only focuses on how you treat yourself but also on your thoughts and how you feel about yourself.
3. When you love yourself, you can love others.
4. Self-love is vital so that you do not neglect your own needs.

Answer:

The following are examples of what self-love looks like:

- Accepting your imperfections
- Recognizing your strengths
- Pursuing your interests and goals and having a vision for your life
- Holding yourself accountable
- Meeting your own needs
- Doing positive self-talk
- Forgiving yourself
- Not allowing others to take advantage of you
- Not allowing others to abuse you
- Asking for help when needed
- Being with others who support and inspire you
- Valuing your feelings
- Making better choices
- Treating yourself well

Play Youtube.com Video ("The Greatest Love of All" by Whitney/Celine, 5 minutes 22 seconds)

What does the Bible say about "self-love?"

Scriptures:

A. I praise you, for I am fearfully and wonderfully made. (Psalms 139:13–14) (ESV)

B. For no one ever hated his flesh but nourishes and cherishes it. (Ephesians 5:29) (ESV)

C. And above all, this put-on love, which binds everything together in perfect harmony. (Colossians 3:14) (ESV)

D. Before I formed you in the womb, I knew you before you were born. (Jeremiah 1:5) (ESV)

E. Just as He chose us in Him before the foundation before the world. (Ephesians 1:4) (ESV)

F. We are His workmanship created in Christ, Jesus for g woodwork. (Ephesians 2:10) (ESV)

Class Discussion Questions: (Use an electronic device or paper)

What are the good things that you like about yourself? What are the things you honor and appreciate about who you are? What are your strengths? What do others understand about you? Are there any good qualities your friends possess that you wish you had? How would your friends describe you?

Read the list out loud in front of someone you trust or in front of a mirror. Recite the list so that the words stick. Words paint a picture and help you hear it out loud and believe in it.

Examples:

"I love my confidence."

"I love that I know how to be a friend."

"I love my ability to be respectful."

Celebrate your strengths. Call those things that are not as if they were (Romans 4:17 KJV). Say the things that God says about you. And the Lord shall make thee the head and not the tail (Deuteronomy 28:13). I will praise you for I am fearfully and wonderfully made (Psalms 139:14 KJV). Yet in all these things, we are more than conquerors through Him who loved us (Romans 8:37 NKJV).

Before the foundation of the world, God knew you. God mapped out His plan for your life, just as it says in Jeremiah 29:11. I know the plans that I have for you to prosper, do good, and have a future and a hope. It's already done and, nothing can stop your destiny. Did you know that you were chosen before the foundation of the world? God determined our end from the beginning. He already has your life worked out for you; all you have to do is just follow it.

You were created out of love, not for failure or for defeat. The scripture declares that you are fearfully and wonderfully made. Priscilla Shirer states in her book Fervent that the enemy (Satan) would like you to believe that God does not love you and will not help you. That you are living in a state of defeat. Your defenses down. Your resolve weak and flimsy. It makes you wonder, then, why all we often tend to see when we look at ourselves are . . . flaws, inadequacies, failures, weaknesses. The enemy wants you to suffer from a case of mistaken identity." (Priscilla Shirer, p.57)

If we see God, the one who created us out of love, as being the potter and us being the clay, then we will have more love for ourselves and God. God did not make a mistake when He created us. "More skilled than any earthly artist, God had pre-planned each of His children, choosing our shape and form, crafting us for our life's calling before He colored in a single stroke of our lives. "God plotted and framed the very family into which we would be born. (Jennifer Gerelds, p.78) God did not make a mistake when He created you. When you look at yourself, do you like what you see? We find rest when we remember we are God's work in progress."(Jennifer Gerelds, p.79). I am certain that God, who began the good work within you, will continue His work until it is finally finished on the day when Christ Jesus returns. (Philippians 1:6 NLT)

Ending Prayer/Prayer of Salvation:

Prayer of Salvation:

Dear Jesus, please forgive me for all my sins. I believe you died on the Cross and rose again. Come into my life and help me trust and follow you. I accept you as Lord and Savior over my life; in Jesus's name, Amen.

Weekly Class Activities Agenda

(RECOMMENDED TIME: 1 HOUR):

- Attendance (2 minutes)
- Good News (2 minutes)
- Beginning Prayer (2 minutes)
- Discuss Virtual Class Norms (2 minutes)
- Panel Introduction (2 minutes)
- Acrostic Poem for Self-Respect (10 minutes)
- Discussion Topic Question(s) (20 minutes)
- Class Discussion Question(s)
- Plan of Salvation (5 minutes)
- Ending Prayer (2 minutes)
- Class Evaluation (Google Form) (5 minutes)
- Affirmations (3 minutes)

How to Teach?

The teacher will follow the Weekly Class Activities Agenda.

Beginning Prayer

Dear God bless this day that you have made and help us to rejoice and be glad in it. Give us clarity of mind, revelation of who you are, wisdom, knowledge, and discernment on how to apply each lesson to our life. Guide and direct our footsteps and show us your will and purpose for our life. Thank you for blessing us so that we may be a blessing to others. In Jesus name, Amen.

Purpose: This lesson aims to help girls increase their confidence, behave with grace, honor, and dignity.

Key Terms: value, belief, dignity, glorify.

Week 5

Self-Respect

Self-respect is pride and confidence in oneself, a feeling that one is behaving with honor and dignity.

Select the best example of a girl showing self-respect:

1. Vivian was in the locker room with the other basketball team members. The team members asked Vivian to hang out with them at the bridge after school to try the new flavored Vape Pen that Amber stole from the gas station. Vivian told them that she did not want to hang out and smoke with them because it is terrible for their health, and that they could still get suspended if caught even though they would be off campus. One of the girls laughed and shouted, "Well, if we die, then the principal cannot suspend us."
2. Julie Ann and Adriana were texting each other about meeting over at Michael's house to party. His parents were away for a conference, and his older brother was in charge. There would be plenty of food, drinks, and loud music. Julie Ann texted Adriana back and gave her the directions to Michael's house and said that she would meet her there after school.

Answer: 1

Discussion Topic Question: What is self-respect? How can you earn the respect of others?

Instruction: Provide thirty seconds of wait time for the girls to respond to the question. If no one answers, then the panel and/or coordinator will respond to the question.

Answer:

You can earn respect from others by keeping your promises. Stop apologizing.

Respect that other people's time is just as important. When you do this, they will respect you. Being on time shows that you value the other person and respect their time. Stop gossiping about others. Be genuine. Let others talk about themselves and be right. You're not always going to be correct, and you're not the best at everything. Every person we meet can teach us something. Have some moral code and set boundaries. What do you believe in? What is important to you and why? Believe in you and your ideas. Speak up when someone is mistreating you. Have an opinion on important topics. Listen more and talk less. That is why we have two ears and one mouth.

Activity: Create an acrostic poem with the letters from the word "self-respect."

Self-Reflection Questions

Whom do you respect and why?

What can you learn from the people you respect?

What does the Bible say about "self-respect?"

Scriptures:

You were bought with a price. So, glorify God in your body. (1 Corinthians 6:20) (ESV)

A. Do your best to present yourself to God as one approved, a worker who has no need to be ashamed. (2 Timothy 2:15) (ESV)

B. For we are his workmanship, created in Christ Jesus, for good works, which God prepared beforehand. (Ephesians 2:10) (ESV)

Ending Prayer/Prayer of Salvation:

Prayer of Salvation:

Dear Jesus, please forgive me for all my sins. I believe you died on the Cross and rose again. Come into my life and help me trust and follow you. I accept you as Lord and Savior over my life; in Jesus's name, Amen.

Weekly Class Activities Agenda

(RECOMMENDED TIME: 1 HOUR):

- Attendance (2 minutes)
- Good News (2 minutes)
- Beginning Prayer (2 minutes)
- Discuss Virtual Class Norms (2 minutes)
- Panel Introduction (2 minutes)
- Song Video ("The Champion" by Carrie Underwood/Ludacris) (Video Time 3:25)
- Discussion Topic Question(s) (20 minutes)
- Class Discussion Question(s) or Self-Reflection Question (email) (10 minutes)
- Plan of Salvation (5 minutes)
- Ending Prayer (2 minutes)
- Class Evaluation (Google Form) (10 minutes)
- Affirmations (3 minutes)

How to Teach?

The instructor will follow the Weekly Class Activities Agenda.

Beginning Prayer

Dear God bless this day that you have made and help us to rejoice and be glad in it. Give us clarity of mind, revelation of who you are, wisdom, knowledge, and discernment on how to apply each lesson to our life. Guide and direct our footsteps and show us your will and purpose for our life. Thank you for blessing us so that we may be a blessing to others. In Jesus name, Amen.

Purpose: This lesson aims to develop integrity through having solid morals, boundaries, and principles.

Key Terms: integrity, morals, ethics, principles, secure, treacherous

Week 6

Self-Integrity

Integrity is being honest and having strong morals and principles.

Select the best example that displays integrity:

1. Darlene stole a $10 bill from her mother's purse so that she could have money to attend the movies after school. Whenever her mother mentioned that she was missing $10 from her wallet, Darlene just kept silent and went to her bedroom.
2. Sarah was running late for school, and her dad was asleep. She reached into his wallet and took out a $20 bill to pay for her school pictures. After Sarah arrived at school, she contacted her dad over the phone to explain the missing money. She told him that she would pay him back on payday. He told her to keep the money and put it in the bank for her college fund; he thanked her for calling him and being honest.

Answer: 2

Discussion Topic Question: How do you develop self-integrity?

Instruction: Provide thirty seconds of wait time for the girls to respond to the question. If no one answers, then the panel and/or coordinator will respond to the question.

Answer:

Self-integrity is the practice of being honest and showing a consistent and uncompromising adherence to strong moral and ethical principles and values. It is the honesty and truthfulness or accuracy of one's actions. Examine your morals and ethics. Stand up for what you believe. When you make promises, keep them. A commitment is the first part of a decision, a responsibility that you have chosen to take on. Surround yourself with others who have the same morals and ethics that you have. Nona Jones writes that while the way we behave creates our reputation, our behavior is an extension of our character. She modulated her behavior on the basis of the external validation that she received from teachers, and she continues by saying that the root of that change wasn't a personal desire to be better; it was the insecurity of wanting, and needing, attention.

Proverbs 23:7 says, "As a man thinks in his heart, so is he." (NKJV)

Play Youtube.com Video ("The Champion" by Carrie Underwood/Ludacris, 3 minutes 26 seconds)

What does the Bible say about "self-integrity?

Scriptures:

A. Whoever walks in integrity walks securely, but he who makes his ways crooked will be found out. (Proverbs 10:9) (ESV)
B. Better is a poor man who walks in his integrity than a rich man who is crooked in his ways. (Proverbs 28:6) (ESV)
C. The integrity of the upright guides them, but the crookedness of the treacherous destroys them. (Proverbs 11:3) (ESV)

Ending Prayer/Prayer of Salvation:

Prayer of Salvation:

Dear Jesus, please forgive me for all my sins. I believe you died on the Cross and rose again. Come into my life and help me trust and follow you. I accept you as Lord and Savior over my life; in Jesus's name, Amen.

Weekly Class Activities Agenda

(RECOMMENDED TIME: 1 HOUR):

- Attendance (2 minutes)
- Good News (2 minutes)
- Beginning Prayer (2 minutes)
- Discuss Virtual Class Norms (2 minutes)
- Panel Introduction (2 minutes)
- Song Video ("See You Again" by Wiz Khalifa/Charlie Puth) (Video Time 3:57)
- Discussion Topic Question(s) (20 minutes)
- Class Discussion Question(s)
- Plan of Salvation (5 minutes)
- Ending Prayer (2 minutes)
- Class Evaluation (Google Form) (10 minutes)
- Affirmations (3 minutes)

How to Teach?

The instructor will follow the Weekly Class Activities Agenda.

Beginning Prayer

Dear God bless this day that you have made and help us to rejoice and be glad in it. Give us clarity of mind, revelation of who you are, wisdom, knowledge, and discernment on how to apply each lesson to our life. Guide and direct our footsteps and show us your will and purpose for our life. Thank you for blessing us so that we may be a blessing to others. In Jesus name, Amen.

Purpose: This lesson aims to define the qualities that make a good and loyal friend.

Key Terms: qualities, loyal, gracious, seasoned, wrathful, rejection

Week 7

Making and Maintaining Friendships

A friendship is a close relationship with another person, male and/or female.

Select the best example for the story that shows a friendship:

1. Maritza and Olga enjoy going shopping on Fridays. After shopping, they go to the movies. Maritza likes eating the buttered popcorn with peanuts and she always orders a Slurpee. Olga likes red vines and a hot dog with mustard. The girls are now twelve and have been friends since kindergarten.
2. Jada and Amber both go to the Lakewood Mall on Fridays after school. Jada goes with Amber but ditches her to go and hang out with her boyfriend. Amber goes with Jada so that Jada's mother will think they are at the mall shopping together.

Answer: 1

Discussion Topic Question: What are some of the qualities that make a person a friend?

Instruction: Provide thirty seconds of wait time for the girls to respond to the question. If no one answers, then the panel and/or coordinator will respond to the question.

Answer:

Some of the qualities that make up a great friend are trustworthiness, honesty, dependability, loyalty, good attentiveness, humor, and the ability to encourage or empathize.

In Romans 12:18-19, God instructs us to live peaceably with all men. When I am praying about my relationships, I ask God to help me show love, kindness, forgive, to be able to laugh and have fun. We need friendships to help us fulfill our purpose here on earth. Friendships help us celebrate good times and provide support for during the bad times. Friends should push you to be the best version by being a positive influence in your life. Friendships can also help foster your purpose in life and promote feelings of self-worth. Sun Tzu has been credited with the phrase, "Keep your friends close; keep your enemies closer." In other words, you will be safer if you know more about your enemies thatn about your friends. In her book, "Untangled" Dr. Damour calls them frenemies. "Frenemy can be a term used to capture a variety of conflicted, relationships, including that with a peer who can be lots of fun except when she is being competitive rotten." (Dr. Lisa Damour, p.58) The term frenemy will only be used when the friendship is not going well.

"Being and having a friend encompasses and requires the infusion of a lot of ingredients; hard work, honesty, forgiveness, respect, love and prayer." (Dr. Victory Vernon, p.102)

Play Youtube.com Video ("See You Again" by Wiz Khalifa/Charlie Puth, 3 minutes 57 seconds)

What does the Bible say about "friendships?"

Scriptures:

A. Do not be unequally yoked with unbelievers. (2 Corinthians 6:14) (ESV)

B. Let your speech always be gracious, seasoned with salt so that you may know how. (Colossians 4:6) (ESV)

C. A friend loves at all times, and a brother is born for adversity. (Proverbs 17:17) (ESV)

D. A man of many companions may come to ruin, but there is a friend who sticks closer than a brother. (Proverbs 18:24) (ESV)

E. Make no friendship with a man given to anger nor go with a wrathful man. (Proverbs 22:24-25) (ESV)

Self-Reflection: What are some of the good qualities/characteristics that my friends exhibit?

Answer:

My friends' good characteristics are trustworthiness, honesty, dependability, transparency, compassion, loyalty and empathy. They make me laugh and are non-judgmental, supportive, etc.

Ending Prayer/Prayer of Salvation:

Prayer of Salvation:

Dear Jesus, please forgive me for all my sins. I believe you died on the Cross and rose again. Come into my life and help me trust and follow you. I accept you as Lord and Savior over my life; in Jesus's name, Amen.

Weekly Class Activities Agenda

(RECOMMENDED TIME: 1 HOUR):

- Attendance (2 minutes)
- Good News (2 minutes)
- Beginning Prayer (2 minutes)
- Discuss Virtual Class Norms (2 minutes)
- Panel Introduction (2 minutes)
- Song Video ("Don't You Worry 'Bout A Thing" by Tori Kelly) (Video Time 3:11)
- Discussion Topic Question(s) (20 minutes)
- Class Discussion Question(s) or Self-Reflection Question (email) (10 minutes)
- Plan of Salvation (5 minutes)
- Ending Prayer (2 minutes)
- Class Evaluation (Google Form) (10 minutes)
- Affirmations (3 minutes)

How to Teach?

The teacher will follow the Weekly Class Activities Agenda.

Beginning Prayer

Dear God bless this day that you have made and help us to rejoice and be glad in it. Give us clarity of mind, revelation of who you are, wisdom, knowledge, and discernment on how to apply each lesson to our life. Guide and direct our footsteps and show us your will and purpose for our life. Thank you for blessing us so that we may be a blessing to others. In Jesus name, Amen.

Purpose: The purpose of this lesson is to help you become aware of who you are.

Key Terms: discernment, entourage, stature, false metric narrative, adorn, apparel, renewing.

Week 8

Individuality

Individuality is a quality or character that distinguishes you from another person.

Select the best example that displays being an individual:

1. Sara and Cara are twin sisters who are in the sixth grade at Chandler Middle School. Sara and Cara enjoy dressing alike and spending time together every day.
2. Stormy and Rain are twin sisters who do not look alike, nor do they like dressing alike. They both have different friends. Stormy loves chocolate ice cream, and Rain loves bubble-gum ice cream. They each have their own rooms at home. When home, they like talking and watching movies together, but they enjoy having their space when possible. Stormy dyed her hair pink and purple, and Rain likes wearing her hair in red and blue dreadlocks.

Answer: 2

Discussion Topic Questions: How are you different or unique from your friends? What makes you an individual?

Instruction: Provide thirty seconds of wait time for the girls to respond to the question. If no one answers, then the panel and/or coordinator will respond to the question.

Answer:

I am different from my friends because God made me unique. I have unique fingerprints and dental work. My spiritual gifts and talents are different. My goals, dreams, and vision for my life are different. My interests, looks, and attitude are different too.

Discussion Question: How to become a better individual?

Homework Question: Why is it important to know that you are fearfully and wonderfully made by God?

Answer:

It is essential to know that you were created and designed for a purpose in love. You are not a mistake. You were designed with an excellent need for your creator, God. Even though the blueprints of you are like other human beings, they are not precisely the same. You are a unique individual, and no one else on the planet is the same as you are. You may not feel as though you know you have a purpose because all you see are your weaknesses. We all have flaws that make us feel as though we are of no use. Weaknesses keep us humble and dependent on God, and His grace is sufficient to cover our shortcomings. God's power is made perfect in our weaknesses.

Self-Reflection: How can I positively promote my individuality?

Answer:

I can promote my individuality by getting to know who I am and what I like, by spending more time with myself, and accepting myself and focusing more on improving my internal qualities instead of my external attributes. My superficial traits will change or fade, but who I am inside will always be who I am.

Play Youtube.com Video ("Don't You Worry 'Bout A Thing" by Tori Kelly, 3 minutes 11 seconds)

What does the Bible say about "individuality?"

Scriptures:

A. Why even the hairs on your head are all numbered. Fear not, you are of more value than many sparrows. (Luke 12:7) (ESV)

B. But even the hairs of your head are all numbered. (Matthew 10:30) (ESV)

C. So, God created man in His own image; in the image of God, he created him; male and female He created them. (Genesis 1:27) (ESV)

Ending Prayer/Prayer of Salvation:

Prayer of Salvation:

Dear Jesus, please forgive me for all my sins. I believe you died on the Cross and rose again. Come into my life and help me trust and follow you. I accept you as Lord and Savior over my life; in Jesus's name, Amen.

Weekly Class Activities Agenda

(RECOMMENDED TIME: 1 HOUR)

- Attendance (2 minutes)
- Good News (2 minutes)
- Beginning Prayer (2 minutes)
- Discuss Virtual Class Norms (2 minutes)
- Panel Introduction (2 minutes)
- Written Expression (Write a short response) (20 minutes)
- Discussion Topic Question(s) (15 minutes)
- Class Discussion Question(s)
- Plan of Salvation (5 minutes)
- Ending Prayer (2 minutes)
- Class Evaluation (Google Form) (5 minutes)
- Affirmations (3 minutes)

How to Teach?

The teacher will follow the Weekly Class Activities Agenda.

Beginning Prayer

Dear God bless this day that you have made and help us to rejoice and be glad in it. Give us clarity of mind, revelation of who you are, wisdom, knowledge, and discernment on how to apply each lesson to our life. Guide and direct our footsteps and show us your will and purpose for our life. Thank you for blessing us so that we may be a blessing to others. In Jesus name, Amen.

Purpose: The purpose of this lesson is to show you how to impact and influence other people's lives positively.

Key Terms: captive, philosophy, deceit, moral, abstain.

Week 9

Influence

Influence is how you affect another person's character or development.

Select the best example that shows a person having a positive influence on someone else.

1. Myra has a six-year-old sister whom she helps get ready in the mornings before school. She fixes her sister Tyra's breakfast and makes her snack and lunch. Tyra knows that Myra loves her because Myra places a colored Post-it in her lunch box daily with a smiley face.
2. Jessie has a seven-year-old brother who loves to follow her around at home. Jessie locks him out of her room and hardly spends any time with him because she is too busy. She tells him, "Go away, you little creep."

Answer: 1

Discussion Topic Question: How can you make a positive influence on someone's life?

Instruction: Provide thirty seconds of wait time for the girls to respond to the question. If no one answers, then the panel and/or coordinator will respond to the question.

Answer:

Suppose you want to be a positive influence or a leader in someone's life and have a positive attitude. Lead by example, be creative, be compassionate, and learn how to deal with negativity.

Activity: Write a short response on "Who has been a significant influence in your life?"

What does the Bible say about being a positive "influence" on others?

Scriptures:

A. Do not be deceived: "Bad company ruins good morals". (1 Corinthians 15:33) (ESV)
B. B. See to it that no one takes us captive by philosophy and empty deceit. (Colossians 2:8) (ESV)
C. Abstain from every form of evil. (1 Thessalonians 5:22) (ESV)

Ending Prayer/Prayer of Salvation:

Prayer of Salvation:

Dear Jesus, please forgive me for all my sins. I believe you died on the Cross and rose again. Come into my life and help me trust and follow you. I accept you as Lord and Savior over my life; in Jesus's name, Amen.

Weekly Class Activities Agenda

(RECOMMENDED TIME: 1 HOUR):

- Attendance (2 minutes)
- Ice Breakers/Good News/Sharing (2 minutes)
- Beginning Prayer (2 minutes)
- Discuss/Virtual and/or Classroom Norms (2 minutes) (Examples in Attachments)
- Panel/Lesson Introduction (2 minutes) (Virtual Learning only)
- Song Video ("Flaws" with lyrics by Kierra Sheard) (Video Time 3:16)
- Discussion Topic Question(s) (20 minutes)
- Plan of Salvation (As needed 2–5 minutes)
- Ending Prayer (2 minutes)
- Class Evaluation (Google Form) (10 minutes)
- Affirmations (3 minutes) (Students provide positive words to others)
- Prayer Cards (Filled out by the students for personal prayers)
- Self-Reflection Cards (Filled out by the students)

Beginning Prayer

Dear God bless this day that you have made and help us to rejoice and be glad in it. Give us clarity of mind, revelation of who you are, wisdom, knowledge, and discernment on how to apply each lesson to our life. Guide and direct our footsteps and show us your will and purpose for our life. Thank you for blessing us so that we may be a blessing to others. In Jesus name, Amen.

Purpose: This lesson aims to determine if you are depressed and when you should reach out to someone for help.

Key Terms: depression, dismayed.

Week 10

Depression

Depression is a mood disorder that causes someone to feel sad or lost. It also involves the body, mood, and thoughts that affect how a person eats, their periods of sleep, and how they think about oneself.

Select the best example that indicates which girl shows signs of being depressed:

1. Rachel asks Jonathan if he completed last night's homework. Jonathan tells Rachel that he does not remember the language arts teacher giving out any assignment. Rachel sighs and tells Jonathan, thank you.
2. Ramona is sitting in the back of the classroom, just staring into space. The teacher contacted Ramona's mother to inform her of the behavior. Ramona's mom will be coming to pick her up from school. Ramona is sorrowful because her Abuela died last night.

Answer: 2

Discussion Topic Question: Have you ever been depressed or anxious? What makes you depressed or anxious?

Instruction: Provide thirty seconds of wait time for the girls to respond to the question. If no one answers, then the panel and/or coordinator will respond to the question for discussion.

Answer:

Some of the things that trigger teen depression include having issues that impact self-esteem, negatively, such as obesity, peer pressure, long-term bullying, and academic problems in school.

Daniel K. Hall- Flavin states that depression can also be clinical. "Clinical depression is usually a more severe form of depression, which is known as major depression or a major depressive disorder. If you experience feelings of sadness, emptiness, or hopelessness, or show signs of loss of interest, have frequent thoughts of death or suicide, or make suicide attempts, please let your parent or guardian know.

Homework Questions:

Who do you reach out to whenever you are depressed?

What are some of the things that make you depressed?

Answer:

Whenever I am depressed, I reach out to a friend(s), teacher(s), parent(s), guardian, or loved one(s). Sometimes, reaching out to a counselor or a therapist is excellent too. Some of the things that can make me depressed or anxious for a short time are losing a loved one, feeling rejected, health problem, weight gain, lack of purpose or direction, loss of a friendship, and/or being stressed. Whenever I feel depressed, I usually exercise, meditate on scripture, or do something positive. I check my diet to see what foods I have been craving and eating that have changed my mood. John Steinbeck wrote, "A problem difficult at night is resolved in the morning after the committee of sleep has worked on it." Joel Osteen says this, "You control what's in your container. You control what you think about and what you choose to allow in."

Play Youtube.com Video ("Lovely Day" by Demi Lovato, 3 minutes 37 seconds)

What does the Bible say about "depression?"

Bible Story Reference: (Read the story of Elijah running away from Ahab and Jezebel and how he became depressed) (1 Kings 19)

Scriptures:

A. When the righteous cry for help, the Lord hears and delivers them out of all their troubles. (Psalms 34:17–18) (ESV)

B. Fear not for I am with you; be not dismayed for I am your God. (Isaiah 41:10) (ESV)

C. Casting all your anxieties on Him because He cares for you. (1 Peter 5:7) (ESV)

Ending Prayer/Prayer of Salvation:

Prayer of Salvation:

Dear Jesus, please forgive me for all my sins. I believe you died on the Cross and rose again. Come into my life and help me trust and follow you. I accept you as Lord and Savior over my life; in Jesus's name, Amen

Weekly Class Activities Agenda

(RECOMMENDED TIME: 1 HOUR):

- Attendance (2 minutes)
- Good News (2 minutes)
- Beginning Prayer (2 minutes)
- Discuss Virtual Class Norms (2 minutes)
- Panel Introduction (2 minutes)
- Self-Reflection (10 minutes)
- Discussion Topic Question(s) (20 minutes)
- Class Discussion Question(s)
- Plan of Salvation (5 minutes)
- Ending Prayer (2 minutes)
- Class Evaluation (Google Form) (10 minutes)
- Affirmations (3 minutes)

How to Teach?

The teacher will follow the Weekly Class Activities Agenda.

Beginning Prayer

Dear God bless this day that you have made and help us to rejoice and be glad in it. Give us clarity of mind, revelation of who you are, wisdom, knowledge, and discernment on how to apply each lesson to our life. Guide and direct our footsteps and show us your will and purpose for our life. Thank you for blessing us so that we may be a blessing to others. In Jesus name, Amen.

Purpose: The purpose of this lesson is to learn how exercise can benefit your body and mood.

Discussion Topic: Exercise

Key Terms: vigorously, enhances, Holy Spirit, mental health, temple.

Week 11

Exercise

Exercise is an activity requiring physical effort which is carried out to maintain or improve health and fitness.

Select the best example that shows how exercising can increase your heart rate.

1. Catarina runs five laps on the field track after school five times a week to increase her endurance and stay in excellent physical shape. On Fridays, at school, she is always energized and enthusiastic about running the mile. Catarina would like to be a personal fitness trainer for celebrities as a career.
2. Today is Friday; the students are given a test in their physical education class to see how fast they can run a mile. Sunny and her friends never run or jog during this time. They are always walking slowly, socializing, and looking at videos on their cellphone.

Answer: 1

Discussion Topic Question: Why is exercise so important for a teenager's health?

Instruction: Provide thirty seconds of wait time for the girls to respond to the question. If no one answers, then the panel and/or coordinator will respond to the question for discussion.

Answer:

Teens should exercise regularly because it helps them maintain physical and mental health. Teenagers should exercise vigorously at least sixty minutes per day. Physical exercise benefits the body's production of endorphins, which are chemicals that improve one's mood. It also enhances creative thinking and learning, which may improve your performance in school. Physical activity reduces the risk of depression, increases self-esteem, helps with sleep, and builds self-confidence.

Exercising also burns calories which can help teens avoid weight gain and develop a lean, toned body. Regular exercising for teens can help reduce type-2 diabetes, stroke, colon cancer, and breast cancer.

Activity: Fill out the Self-Reflection Form and return to the teacher. (10 minutes)

Self-Reflection:

What type of exercises are you involved in regularly? Is there anything prohibiting you from exercising? What? Do you have any health problems that prohibit you from exercising, or do you need to modify an exercise program?

Aerobic exercises quicken your heart rate, and breathing is good for the heart. These are some of the other activities that can get the blood pumping: basketball, hockey, soccer, running, swimming, dancing, tennis, biking, Zumba, stretching, boxing, yoga, skiing, weightlifting, gymnastics, skating, and baseball.

Strength training helps your muscles increase your endurance. Exercising helps reduce stress. Also, muscle burns fat better; the more muscles you have, the more calories you burn. A flexible person has a lower chance of getting sprains and strained muscles.

What does the Bible say about "exercise?"

Scriptures:

A. For a while, bodily training is of some value; godliness is vital in every way, as it holds promise. (1 Timothy 4:8) (ESV)

B. Or do you not know that your body is a temple of the Holy Spirit within you. (1 Corinthians 6:19–20) (ESV)

C. I can do all things through Him who strengthens me. (Philippians 4:13) (ESV)

D. Stop seeing giants around you. Begin to see yourself conquering everything.

Ending Prayer/Prayer of Salvation:

Prayer of Salvation:

Dear Jesus, please forgive me for all my sins. I believe you died on the Cross and rose again. Come into my life and help me trust and follow you. I accept you as Lord and Savior over my life; in Jesus's name, Amen.

Weekly Class Activities Agenda

(RECOMMENDED TIME: 1 HOUR):

Attendance (2 minutes)

Good News (2 minutes)

Beginning Prayer (2 minutes)

Discuss Virtual Class Norms (2 minutes)

Panel Introduction (2 minutes)

Song Video ("Happy" by Pharrell) (Video Time 3:54)

Discussion Topic Question(s) (20 minutes)

Class Discussion Question(s)

Plan of Salvation (5 minutes)

Ending Prayer (2 minutes)

Class Evaluation (Google Form) (10 minutes)

Affirmations (3 minutes)

How to Teach?

The teacher will follow the Weekly Class Activities Agenda.

Beginning Prayer

Dear God bless this day that you have made and help us to rejoice and be glad in it. Give us clarity of mind, revelation of who you are, wisdom, knowledge, and discernment on how to apply each lesson to our life. Guide and direct our footsteps and show us your will and purpose for our life. Thank you for blessing us so that we may be a blessing to others. In Jesus name, Amen.

Purpose: The purpose of this lesson is to show you how your attitude can affect your day.

Key Terms: attitude, gratitude, thermostat, thermometer

Week 12

Attitude

Attitude is a feeling about something or someone.

Select the best example of a student displaying a negative attitude.

1. Yesterday, Mr. Rivera, the Science teacher, selected Felicia to present today. Felicia would be giving a presentation on using a fidget spinner to explore the laws of motion. Whenever Mr. Rivera calls on Felicia for the exhibition, she stares at him, trembling. Felicia informs the instructor that the assignment has not been completed. Mr. Rivera tells Felicia that she will still have to present and be ready for tomorrow. Felicia says, "Whatever," and continues talking to a classmate."
2. In front of the class, Maria gives her presentation on building a generator from scratch to produce electricity. The teacher and students were impressed with the production. Maria enjoyed working on the project because it challenged her abilities and technical skills. It also gave her clarity on a possible career after high school. She thought about following in the footsteps like other family members and becoming an engineer.

Answer: 2

Discussion Topic Questions: Why is it good to have a positive attitude about life? How should you begin your day if you want it to go well?

Instruction: Provide thirty seconds of wait time for the girls to respond to the question. If no one answers, then the panel and/or coordinator will respond to the question for discussion.

Answer:

It is good to have a positive attitude so that you can cope more easily with daily events. Positivity helps you be more optimistic about life, and it makes it easier to avoid worrying and thinking. A positive attitude can lead to success and a happier life.

These are some of the things that you can do to have a more positive attitude in life:

- Focusing on the good things
- Practicing gratitude
- Practicing positive self-talk
- Laughing a lot
- Laughing at yourself more
- Spending time with positive people
- Beginning your day with a positive thought
- Seeing the glass as half full instead of half empty

In one of Joel Osteen sermons, he spoke about how studies show that your attitude will have a greater impact on your success in life than your IQ.

You can be the most intelligent person in the world, but because of your attitude or bad mood, no one will want to be your friend or hire you to work for them.

Play Youtube.com Video ("Happy" by Pharrell, 3 minutes 54 seconds)

What does the Bible say about having a "positive attitude?"

Scriptures:

A. You will be above only and not beneath. You will always be at the top. (Deuteronomy 28:13) (ESV)

B. Refuse to accept any other type of thinking. Be a thermostat and not a thermometer. Set the thermostat of your attitude to "Above Only."

C. I can do all things through Jesus Christ, who strengthens me. (Philippians 4:13) (ESV)

D. Stop seeing giants around you. Start seeing the giant inside of you. Begin to see yourself conquering everything!

Ending Prayer/Prayer of Salvation:

Prayer of Salvation:

Dear Jesus, please forgive me for all my sins. I believe you died on the Cross and rose again. Come into my life and help me trust and follow you. I accept you as Lord and Savior over my life; in Jesus's name, Amen.

Weekly Class Activities Agenda

(RECOMMENDED TIME: 1 HOUR):

- Attendance (2 minutes)
- Good News (2 minutes)
- Beginning Prayer (2 minutes)
- Discuss Virtual Class Norms (2 minutes)
- Panel Introduction (2 minutes)
- Song Video ("Roar" by Katie Perry) (Video Time 4:29)
- Discussion Topic Question(s) (20 minutes)
- Class Discussion Question(s)
- Plan of Salvation (5 minutes)
- Ending Prayer (2 minutes)
- Class Evaluation (Google Form) (7 minutes)
- Affirmations (3 minutes)

How to Teach?

The teacher will follow the Weekly Class Activities Agenda.

Beginning Prayer

Dear God bless this day that you have made and help us to rejoice and be glad in it. Give us clarity of mind, revelation of who you are, wisdom, knowledge, and discernment on how to apply each lesson to our life. Guide and direct our footsteps and show us your will and purpose for our life. Thank you for blessing us so that we may be a blessing to others. In Jesus name, Amen.

Purpose: This lesson aims to help you become more secure and confident with who you are.

Key Terms: cast, insecurity, supplication, thanksgiving

Week 13

Insecurity

Insecurity is the lack of confidence.

Select the best example of insecurity:

1. Today is the day that Cynthia will join the nutrition and weight-loss class after school. The first step is that the girls must weigh themselves and put the information into the Fitness Tracker. Cynthia refuses to weigh herself in front of the other girls. She tells the teacher that she will complete the activity at home tonight. Cynthia does not want the other girls to know how much she weighs. The girls may body-shame or tell others at school.
2. Whenever the teacher asks for a volunteer to be weighed, North raises her hand and stands on the scale. North has a small built and weighs 105 pounds. She is five feet, five inches tall. She is the girl whom all the others would love to hate because she has a high metabolism and can eat anything and not gain weight. The girls do not know that North has brain cancer, exercises regularly, and must take medication. It is easy to judge a person by how they look instead of getting to know them.

Answer: 1

Discussion Topic Questions: What makes you feel secure or confident about yourself? What is the one thing that makes you feel insecure?

Instruction: Provide thirty seconds of wait time for the girls to respond to the question. If no one answers, then the panel and/or coordinator will respond to the question.

Answer:

Some of the things that make me feel secure or confident are knowing that God loves me family, friends, love, self-acceptance, affirmations and to know that I am fearfully and wonderfully made by God.

Answer:

Some of the things that make me feel insecure are my physical features, not smart enough, failure, frequent criticism, lack of self- acceptance, and not feeling valued or loved. When we don't feel loved, we feel insecure because everyone wants to be loved or validated. As humans we were made to connect with others and live in community together.

These are some of the reasons that R.C. Blakes Jr. gives why girls are insecure is because they were trained to be. He continues to state that insecurity is not a built-in character trait. It is a conditioned behavior. Somebody taught them to feel insecure.

Joyce Meyer writes that are feelings of insecurity and lack of self- confidence are symptoms of fear and believing lies about ourselves that is brought on by the devil in our thoughts. To overcome these negative thoughts, we are encouraged to renew our mind say and believe the things that God says about us that are true. "Renewing the mind takes time and work. The only thing that overturns the lies we believe is the truth of God's Word." (Joyce Meyer, p.37)

Play Youtube.com Video ("Roar" by Katy Perry, 4 minutes 29 seconds)

What does the Bible say about "insecurity?"

Scriptures:

A. You are altogether beautiful, my love; there is no flaw in you. (Song of Solomon 4:7) (ESV)

B. Do not be anxious about anything, but in everything by prayer and supplication with thanksgiving, let your requests be made known to God. (Philippians 4:6) (ESV)

C. And you will know the truth and the truth shall set you free. (John 8:32) (ESV)

D. You will be secure because there is hope, you will look about you and take your rest in safety. You will lie down, with no one to make you afraid. (Job 11:18–19) (ESV)

Self-Reflection:

Think about the things that make you insecure, pray, and cast that care upon God. God does not make us feel insecure. Insecurity comes from negative things that others have said about you. The enemy also places negative thoughts in our thinking to make us doubt our self-worth.

Ending Prayer/Prayer of Salvation:

Prayer of Salvation:

Dear Jesus, please forgive me for all my sins. I believe you died on the Cross and rose again. Come into my life and help me trust and follow you. I accept you as Lord and Savior over my life; in Jesus's name, Amen.

Weekly Class Activities Agenda

(RECOMMENDED TIME: 1 HOUR)

Attendance (2 minutes)

Good News (2 minutes)

Beginning Prayer (2 minutes)

Discuss Virtual Class Norms (2 minutes)

Activity (Responsibility Constructed Response Questions) (10 minutes)

Panel Introduction (2 minutes)

Discussion Topic Question(s) (20 minutes)

Class Discussion Question(s)

Plan of Salvation (5 minutes)

Ending Prayer (2 minutes)

Class Evaluation (Google Form) (10 minutes)

Affirmations (3 minutes)

How to Teach?

The teacher will follow the Weekly Class Activities Agenda.

Beginning Prayer

Dear God bless this day that you have made and help us to rejoice and be glad in it. Give us clarity of mind, revelation of who you are, wisdom, knowledge, and discernment on how to apply each lesson to our life. Guide and direct our footsteps and show us your will and purpose for our life. Thank you for blessing us so that we may be a blessing to others. In Jesus name, Amen.

Purpose: This lesson aims to teach the students why being a responsible person is essential.

Key Terms: accountability, consequences, heartily, responsibility

Week 14

Responsibility

Responsibility is the ability to do something without being told or asked; you also accept blame for your actions.

Select the best example of a girl exhibiting responsibility:

1. Today is the day that Janice's mother begins working as a doctor at the hospital. Janice's dad is resting because he worked four days in a row as fire chief for the Los Angeles County Fire Department. Janice's responsibility is to take Jumanji, their rottweiler dog, out for a walk before she leaves for school. Janice receives a text from Robert, a friend, and she responds to the text. She grabs her black hoodie jacket and is out the door, leaving Jumanji in the living room without food or water to drink.
2. Every day, Cheyenne goes straight home after cheerleading practice. She puts away her books and changes her clothes. Next, Cheyenne gets a plastic bag, gloves, and a pooper scooper to walk their dog, Thunder, a massive, muscular-built bull mastiff. After walking him, she takes him to the dog park to socialize with the other dogs. Thunder always enjoys playing with the other dogs, especially Lola, the French terrier.

Answer: 2

Discussion Topic Question: Why should teens be held responsible for their actions?

Instruction: Provide thirty seconds of wait time for the girls to respond to the question. If no one answers, then the panel and/or coordinator will respond to the question for discussion.

Answer:

Teens should be held responsible or accountable for their actions because it helps prepare them for the future. In real life, you are held accountable for your actions. If you speed through a neighborhood and get a speeding ticket, you must pay for the ticket. Your parent or guardian should not pay it for you. Suppose the teen doesn't study for an exam and gets a failing grade. Let them deal with the failing grade or retake the exam for a better grade. This way, teens will learn how to take responsibility for their actions and deal with the consequences. It allows them to own up to their mistakes and teaches them the difference between right and wrong.

Constructed Response Question
(Have the students write 3-5 sentences to the question below)

How can we make teens more responsible?

Answer:

We can hold teens more responsible by holding them accountable for their homework, cleaning their room, cleaning up after themselves, washing dishes, and washing clothes. Teens should also be held accountable for their actions. If they lose something through carelessness, they should pay for a replacement or work to earn money to pay for it.

Activity: Answer the Constructed Response Questions.

What does the Bible say about "responsibility?"

Scriptures:

A. For each will have to bear his load. (Galatians 6:5) (ESV)

B. Whatever you do, work heartily as for the Lord and not for men. (Colossians 3:23) (ESV)

Ending Prayer/Prayer of Salvation:

Prayer of Salvation:

Dear Jesus, please forgive me for all my sins. I believe you died on the Cross and rose again. Come into my life and help me trust and follow you. I accept you as Lord and Savior over my life; in Jesus's name, Amen.

Weekly Class Activities Agenda

(RECOMMENDED TIME: 1 HOUR):

- Attendance (2 minutes)
- Good News (2 minutes)
- Beginning Prayer (2 minutes)
- Discuss Virtual Class Norms (2 minutes)
- Panel Introduction (2 minutes)
- Song Video ("No Fear" by Kari Jobe) (Video Time 3:10)
- Discussion Topic Question(s) (20 minutes)
- Class Discussion Question(s)
- Plan of Salvation (5 minutes)
- Ending Prayer (2 minutes)
- Class Evaluation (Google Form) (10 minutes)
- Affirmations (3 minutes)

How to Teach?

The teacher will follow the Weekly Class Activities Agenda.

Beginning Prayer

Dear God bless this day that you have made and help us to rejoice and be glad in it. Give us clarity of mind, revelation of who you are, wisdom, knowledge, and discernment on how to apply each lesson to our life. Guide and direct our footsteps and show us your will and purpose for our life. Thank you for blessing us so that we may be a blessing to others. In Jesus name, Amen.

Purpose: To teach the teens how to address their fear(s) or anxieties.

Key Terms: anxiety, dismayed, righteousness.

Week 15

Fear

Fear is to be afraid of something or someone.

Select the best example of fear:

1. When walking to school, Jenna and Magdalena saw a suspicious-looking man walking toward them carrying a knife. They began to tremble before clutching their backpacks and running across the street screaming. A few of the boys in Jenna's math class heard and saw the two girls and ran to their aid. When the suspicious man saw the boys coming towards him, he started running in the opposite direction to get away.
2. Victoria was lying on the bed at night when she felt the bed begin to shake. Her dad called out to her to see if she was okay. He came into her bedroom to inform her that there had been an earthquake. Victoria responded by saying, "Thanks, Dad, and have a good night."

Answer: 1

Fear is a thought process that usually triggers a fight or flight response. Fear is usually imagined but can cause emotional, physiological, and psychological consequences.

Some of the things that make people fearful are snakes, closed in spaces, flying, speaking in front of people, heights, going to the dentist and not having the basic needs to survive.

Discussion Topic Questions:

Is fear real, imaginary or an illusion?

Why are we afraid? Name some things that make you afraid?

Instruction: Provide thirty seconds of wait time for the girls to respond to the question. If no one answers, then the panel and/or coordinator will respond to the question.

Answer:

Yes, fear is real. Fear is a conditioned feeling that may stem from as early as one's childhood. Fear originally was a fight or flight response to stress when confronted with a threatening danger. It then became part of the individual's mind and emotions.

"The only way to live free from fear is to confront it or do it afraid." (Joyce Meyer, p.18)

Many of the fears that we experience are very irrational responses to normal human conditions. People have many fears (real or imagined), but it depends on the individual and their experiences. Sometimes, parents' fears can be transferred to the children. There is nothing to fear except fear itself. Don't let that difficulty become your identity. "Don't get in agreement with the negative." (Joel Osteen, p.79)

Whenever you empty the negative things in your mind, you make more room to entertain your mind's fun and positive things.

Joyce Meyer thinks that fear is a False Evidence Appearing Real because it is rooted in lies that the devil tells us and wants us to believe.

God's Word teaches us that He delivers us from our enemies little by little. (Deuteronomy 7:22)

"I understand that fear can be very controlling. The very thought of confronting fear is fearful." (Joyce Meyer)

Play Youtube.com Video ("No Fear" by Kari Jobe, 3 minutes 10 seconds)

What does the Bible say about "fear?"

Scriptures:

A. Fear not, for I am with you; be not dismayed, for I am your God. I will strengthen you. I will help you; I will uphold you with my righteous right hand. (Isaiah 41:10) (ESV)

B. For God has not given us a spirit of fear but of power, love, and a sound mind. (2 Timothy 1:7) (ESV)

C. I sought the Lord, and He answered me and delivered me from all my fears. (Psalms 34:4) (ESV)

Ending Prayer/Prayer of Salvation:

Prayer of Salvation:

Dear Jesus, please forgive me for all my sins. I believe you died on the Cross and rose again. Come into my life and help me trust and follow you. I accept you as Lord and Savior over my life; in Jesus's name, Amen.

Weekly Class Activities Agenda

(RECOMMENDED TIME: 1 HOUR):

- Attendance (2 minutes)
- Good News (2 minutes)
- Beginning Prayer (2 minutes)
- Discuss Virtual Class Norms (2 minutes)
- Panel Introduction (2 minutes)
- Song Video ("Hit the Refresh" by Voices of Fire) (Video Time 4:41)
- Discussion Topic Question(s) (20 minutes)
- Class Discussion Question(s)
- Plan of Salvation (5 minutes)
- Ending Prayer (2 minutes)
- Class Evaluation (Google Form) (10 minutes)
- Affirmations (3 minutes)

How to Teach?

The teacher will follow the Weekly Class Activities Agenda.

Beginning Prayer

Dear God bless this day that you have made and help us to rejoice and be glad in it. Give us clarity of mind, revelation of who you are, wisdom, knowledge, and discernment on how to apply each lesson to our life. Guide and direct our footsteps and show us your will and purpose for our life. Thank you for blessing us so that we may be a blessing to others. In Jesus name, Amen.

Purpose: The purpose of this lesson is to teach the girls how to exercise their faith.

Key Terms: evidence, faith, substance

Week 16

Faith

Faith is the substance of things hoped for and the evidence of things not seen.

Select the best example of a student exhibiting faith:

1. Nona had applied to ten law schools for enrollment within the last ten months while still in high school. She was waiting for the mail carrier to see if she had received any school acceptance letters. The mail carrier arrived and told Nona that he did not have any mail for her today. She told him thank you and went into the house to assist her mother with dinner. Nona told her mother that she had not received any mail yet but still believed that the answers were on their way.
2. Teri filled out a job application one day at Best Buy to stock their shelves during the Christmas season. She turned in the application to Bill, the manager, and asked him when he would get back to her about the job, and he told her, "In three days." Teri called him for the next three days to see if he had decided on hiring her for the position. Each time he informed her that he would call her as soon as they decided. Teri said bad things about Best Buy and Bill to her family and decided to look elsewhere for employment.

***Answer:*1**

Discussion Topic Question:

What is faith?

What is something that you have prayed for or asked God to do for you?

Instruction: Provide thirty seconds of wait time for the girls to respond to the question. If no one answers, then the panel and/or coordinator will respond to the question for discussion.

Answer:

Faith is a strong belief in God. Faith is complete trust or confidence in something. Faith is the substance of things hoped for and the evidence of something not seen. (Hebrews 11:1 NKJ)

Joyce Meyer says, "I believe the best way to conquer anything is to take one step at a time without thinking about all the other steps you will need to take later."

Play Youtube.com Video ("Hit the Refresh" by Voices of Fire, 4 minutes 41 seconds)

What does the Bible say about "faith?"

Scriptures:

A. And whatever you ask in prayer, you will receive if you have faith. (Matthew 21:22) (ESV)

B. For we walk by faith and not by sight. (2 Corinthians 5:7) (ESV)

C. All things are possible to him who believes. (Mark 9:23) (ESV)

D. Faith is the substance of things hoped for and the evidence of things not seen (Hebrews 11:1) (KJV)

Discussion Topic Question: What are some of the things you pray for that require faith?

Answer:

Some of the things that require exercising your faith are receiving the right classes in high school, being treated with respect, healing of a sickness, getting a job and/or a car, and getting accepted by the right college with a full scholarship.

Ending Prayer/Prayer of Salvation:

Prayer of Salvation:

Dear Jesus, please forgive me for all my sins. I believe you died on the Cross and rose again. Come into my life and help me trust and follow you. I accept you as Lord and Savior over my life; in Jesus's name, Amen.

Weekly Class Activities Agenda

(RECOMMENDED TIME: 1 HOUR):

- Attendance (2 minutes)
- Good News (2 minutes)
- Beginning Prayer (2 minutes)
- Discuss Virtual Class Norms (2 minutes)
- Panel Introduction (2 minutes)
- Song Video ("Help Us to Love" by Tori Kelly/The HamilTones) (Video Time 3:49)
- Discussion Topic Question(s) (20 minutes)
- Class Discussion Question(s)
- Plan of Salvation (5 minutes)
- Ending Prayer (2 minutes)
- Class Evaluation (Google Form) (10 minutes)
- Affirmations (3 minutes)

How to Teach?

The teacher will follow the Weekly Class Activities Agenda.

Beginning Prayer

Dear God bless this day that you have made and help us to rejoice and be glad in it. Give us clarity of mind, revelation of who you are, wisdom, knowledge, and discernment on how to apply each lesson to our life. Guide and direct our footsteps and show us your will and purpose for our life. Thank you for blessing us so that we may be a blessing to others. In Jesus name, Amen.

Purpose: The purpose of this lesson is to develop vital self-love.

Key Terms: abide, affirmation, begotten, eternal, perish, and qualities.

Week 17

Love

Love is an intense feeling for something or someone.

Select the best example that depicts love:

1. Lola went to the shopping mall to purchase a bracelet and earrings for her mother's birthday tomorrow. She used a free online card application to create the birthday card with heart-shaped symbols, streamers, and the words, "Thank you, Mom, for all you have done for the family and me."
2. Tomorrow will be Sidney's little sister's birthday. Kathleen will be turning five years old. Sidney asked her mom to take her to the store to purchase a birthday present for Kathleen. When Sidney got to the shopping mall, she ditched her mom and hooked up with her friends and bought a pair of pink sparkling earrings and blouse to match for Picture Day at school tomorrow. While the family was celebrating Kathleen's birthday, they were waiting on Sidney to present her gift. Sidney handed Kathleen a card that she had made from construction paper. Sidney's mom and the other family members looked dumbfounded. Kathleen hugged Sidney and said, "Thank you, sister."

Answer: 1

Discussion Topic Questions:

How or why should you love yourself? Are you able to help and love your enemies?

Instruction: Provide thirty seconds of wait time for the girls to respond to the question. If no one answers, then the panel and/or coordinator will respond to the question.

Answer:

You can love yourself by providing self-care. Permit yourself to not be perfect. You are giving yourself daily affirmations and treating yourself well. Focus on your positive qualities. Try your best and accept that you've done what you could.

Play Youtube.com Video ("Help Us to Love" by Tori Kelly/The HamilTones, 3 minutes 49 seconds)

What does the Bible say about "self-love?"

Scriptures:

A. Love is patient and kind; love does not envy or boast; it is not arrogant or rude.
B. (1 Corinthians 13:4–8) (ESV)
C. For God so loved the world, that He gave His only begotten Son, that whoever believes in Him should not perish but have eternal life. (John 3:16) (ESV)
D. So now faith, hope and love abide, these three; but the greatest of these is love. (1 Corinthians 13:13) (ESV)

Ending Prayer/Prayer of Salvation:

Prayer of Salvation:

Dear Jesus, please forgive me for all my sins. I believe you died on the Cross and rose again. Come into my life and help me trust and follow you. I accept you as Lord and Savior over my life; in Jesus's name, Amen.

Weekly Class Activities Agenda

(RECOMMENDED TIME: 1 HOUR):

- Attendance (2 minutes)
- Good News (2 minutes)
- Beginning Prayer (2 minutes)
- Discuss Virtual Class Norms (2 minutes)
- Panel Introduction (2 minutes)
- Song Video ("Spread Love" by Take 6) (Video Time 3:51)
- Discussion Topic Question(s) (20 minutes)
- Class Discussion Question(s)
- Plan of Salvation (5 minutes)
- Ending Prayer (2 minutes)
- Class Evaluation (Google Form) (10 minutes)
- Affirmations (3 minutes)

How to Teach?

The teacher will follow the Weekly Class Activities Agenda.

Beginning Prayer

Dear God bless this day that you have made and help us to rejoice and be glad in it. Give us clarity of mind, revelation of who you are, wisdom, knowledge, and discernment on how to apply each lesson to our life. Guide and direct our footsteps and show us your will and purpose for our life. Thank you for blessing us so that we may be a blessing to others. In Jesus name, Amen.

Purpose: This lesson aims to understand how what you listen to can affect your mood and attitude.

Key Terms: affect, community, exposure, harmony, mellow, perception

Week 18

Music

Music is the vocal or instrumental sounds that can be combined to produce harmony or an expression of emotion.

Select the best answer that indicates who has or is listening to appropriate music:

1. Tamera loves to dance and sing. Her parents have taken her phone from her on numerous occasions because she likes listening to music with explicit lyrics, which are inappropriate for her age. Tamera's selection of clothes and friends has changed since she has been wanting to hang out with the popular students at school.

2. Lee Shan Min loves listening to rhythm and blues music whenever she is finished with her homework. Lee sings in the choir at school and plays the keyboard for the church choir. Lee enjoys writing music and playing in the band after school.

Answer: 2

Discussion Topic Question: How does the type of music you listen to affect your attitude?

Instruction: Provide thirty seconds of wait time for the girls to respond to the question. If no one answers, then the panel and/or coordinator will respond to the question for discussion.

Answer:

Music can assist teens in safely exploring ideas and emotions and help them express themselves without words. Exposure to positive influences through music can help the teens learn how to cope with issues and help with appropriate responses to very stressful situations. Further, music can help a team feel as though they belong to a community. Music affects your mood, and listening to some happy or sad music can change how you perceive the world.

Music can change your perception. Music can provide entertainment and distraction from daily problems and can serve to relieve stress and boredom. Music is also great for changing your mood from sad to happy. It can change your attitude from mellow to anger as well, depending on what type of music you listen to. Some Christian hymns and songs are filled with theological text from the bible especially the Psalms. Singing allows us to use both parts of the brain, therefore it can help educate and teach us about the Good News of Jesus Christ. Singing connects us emotionally with God and His goodness towards us. Some songs of celebration have the power to lead us to move our hands, feet, and dance. God commands us to sing praise to the Lord and to sing in His presence. Paul urges us in the book of Ephesians to "be filled with the Holy Spirit, addressing one another in psalms and hymns and spiritual songs, singing and making melody to the Lord with your heart, giving thanks always and for everything to God the Father in the name of our Lord Jesus Christ." (Eph. 5:18-20 ESV)

Play Youtube.com Video ("Spread Love" by Take 6, 3 minutes 51 seconds)

What does the Bible say about "music?"

Scriptures:

A. Sing to Him, sing praises to Him; tell of all His wondrous works! (Psalms 105:2) (ESV)

B. Praise the Lord, for the Lord is good; sing to His name, for it is pleasant! (Psalms 135:3) (ESV)

C. Make a joyful noise unto the Lord, all ye lands. (Psalms 100:1-5) (KJV)

D. Make a joyful noise unto the Lord, all the earth: make a loud noise, and rejoice, and sing praise. (Psalms 98:4) (KJV)

Ending Prayer/Prayer of Salvation:

Prayer of Salvation:

Dear Jesus, please forgive me for all my sins. I believe you died on the Cross and rose again. Come into my life and help me trust and follow you. I accept you as Lord and Savior over my life; in Jesus's name, Amen.

Weekly Class Activities Agenda

(RECOMMENDED TIME: 1 HOUR):

- Attendance (2 minutes)
- Good News (2 minutes)
- Beginning Prayer (2 minutes)
- Discuss Virtual Class Norms (2 minutes)
- Panel Introduction (2 minutes)
- Song Video ("The Prayer" by Andrea Bocelli/Celine Dion) (Video Time 6:30)
- Discussion Topic Question(s) (20 minutes)
- Class Discussion Question(s)
- Plan of Salvation (5 minutes)
- Ending Prayer (2 minutes)
- Class Evaluation (Google Form) (10 minutes)
- Affirmations (3 minutes)

How to Teach?

The teacher will follow the Weekly Class Activities Agenda.

Beginning Prayer

Dear God bless this day that you have made and help us to rejoice and be glad in it. Give us clarity of mind, revelation of who you are, wisdom, knowledge, and discernment on how to apply each lesson to our life. Guide and direct our footsteps and show us your will and purpose for our life. Thank you for blessing us so that we may be a blessing to others. In Jesus name, Amen.

Purpose: The purpose of this lesson is to establish a closer relationship with the Lord through prayer.

Key Terms: circumstances, spiritual

Week 19

Prayer

Prayer is the communication with God. Prayer moves the hand that rules the world.

Select the best example of prayer in the stories:

1. Tomorrow will be the National Day of Prayer. Monica has been contacting classmates to see if they can join outside by the flagpole for prayer.
2. Susanne approaches Dyan at church and tells her that she is nervous about singing in the church play today and asks if she would pray for her to have courage and confidence. Dyan ignores Susanne and walks away.

Answer: 1

Discussion Topic Questions: What is the purpose of prayer? Does God answer every prayer? How does prayer change your life? How do we know what to pray?

Instruction: Provide thirty seconds of wait time for the girls to respond to the question. If no one answers, then the panel and/or coordinator will respond to the question for discussion.

Answer:

Prayer can benefit us in so many ways. The main reason that we should pray to God is because Jesus prayed. Prayer is about developing an intimate relationship with God. Prayer can be used to call upon God to deliver us from or change a difficult situation in life. Sometimes we pray to God and ask what our purpose is in life. In the book of Romans 12:12 the Apostle Paul, informs us to be faithful in prayer. Jesus teaches us how to pray the Lord's Prayer in Matthew 6:9-13. This turns our focus outward to an awareness of who God is and His control and it takes the focus off our requests, our issues, and our sins. It forces us to think about others and the will of God.

The fact is that we become more inclusive than insular when we pray. One thing that you must remember is that when you pray make sure that you pray with the right motives(s). When we pray God looks at what is best for us and how the situation can be used to help us grow stronger and more mature. In other words, God looks at the total picture and how it will affect us others and His purpose. Prayer is an opportunity to spend time with God and understand the heart of God. Remember to pray in faith and believe that you will receive what you ask if it is aligned up according to His will.

Play Youtube.com Video ("The Prayer" by Andrea Bocelli/Celine Dion, 6 minutes 30 seconds)

What does the Bible say about "prayer?"

Scriptures:

A. Do not be anxious about anything, but in everything by prayer and supplication with thanksgiving, let your requests be made known to God. (Philippians 4:6) (ESV)
B. If you abide in me, and my words abide in you, ask whatever you wish, and it will be done for you. (John 15:7) (ESV)
C. Rejoice always, pray without ceasing, give thanks in all circumstances; for this is the will of God in Christ Jesus for you. (I Thessalonians 5:16-18) (ESV)

Ending Prayer/Prayer of Salvation:

Prayer of Salvation:

Dear Jesus, please forgive me for all my sins. I believe you died on the Cross and rose again. Come into my life and help me trust and follow you. I accept you as Lord and Savior over my life; in Jesus's name, Amen.

Weekly Class Activities Agenda

(RECOMMENDED TIME: 1 HOUR):

- Attendance (2 minutes)
- Good News (2 minutes)
- Beginning Prayer (2 minutes)
- Discuss Virtual Class Norms (2 minutes)
- Panel Introduction (2 minutes)
- Activity (Create an Obedience Quote) (15 minutes)
- Discussion Topic Question(s) (20 minutes)
- Class Discussion Question(s)
- Plan of Salvation (5 minutes)
- Ending Prayer (2 minutes)
- Class Evaluation (Google Form) (5 minutes)
- Affirmations (3 minutes)

How to Teach?

The teacher will follow the Weekly Class Activities Agenda.

Beginning Prayer

Dear God bless this day that you have made and help us to rejoice and be glad in it. Give us clarity of mind, revelation of who you are, wisdom, knowledge, and discernment on how to apply each lesson to our life. Guide and direct our footsteps and show us your will and purpose for our life. Thank you for blessing us so that we may be a blessing to others. In Jesus name, Amen.

Purpose: This lesson aims to understand why being obedient can give you a longer life.

Key Terms: authority, compliance, guidance, obedience

Week 20

Obedience

Obedience is one's compliance with an order.

Select the best example of obedience:

1. The Art teacher has warned Lori that her cellphone would be confiscated if it rings again in the classroom. Lori's cellphone rings again, and the teacher asks Lori to place the phone on her desk. Lori tells the teacher that she would rather go to the front office than give up the cellphone. The teacher sends Lori to the front office. The security guard in the front office ends up confiscating Lori's phone, and she will not get it returned to her until the end of the school year.
2. Tanisha is walking in line with the eighth-grade students to the high school when her cellphone rings. The teacher asks Tanisha for the phone and informs her that she will receive it once they return to school. Tanisha gives the cellphone to the teacher.

Answer: 2

Discussion Topic Question: What are some of your struggles as a teen?

Instruction: Provide thirty seconds of wait time for the girls to respond to the question. If no one answers, then the panel and/or coordinator will respond to the question for discussion.

Answer:

Some of the things that we may struggle with are being obedient to those in authority, parents, guardian, teachers, law enforcement, etc., completing chores at home, finishing homework assignments, helping a younger sibling, following parent or guardian rules, and following the school rules.

Perhaps we struggle with obedience because of our pride. Sometimes we can oppose those who are in authority.

Activity: Write down what obedience or obey means to you and use it in a sentence to share.

What does the Bible say about "obedience?"

Scriptures:

A. If you love me, you will keep my commandments. (John 14:15) (ESV)
B. But He said, "Blessed rather are those who hear the word of God and keep it." (Luke 11:28) (ESV)
C. Do not merely listen to the word, and so deceive yourselves. Do what it says. (James 1:22) (NIV)
D. Therefore, everyone who hears these words of mine and puts them into practice is like a wise man who built his house on the rock. (Matthew 7:24) (ESV)
E. Whoever heeds discipline shows the way to life, but whoever ignores correction leads others astray. (Proverbs 10:17) (ESV)
F. Jesus replied, "Anyone who loves me will obey my teaching." (John 14:23) (ESV)

Ending Prayer/Prayer of Salvation:

Prayer of Salvation:

Dear Jesus, please forgive me for all my sins. I believe you died on the Cross and rose again. Come into my life and help me trust and follow you. I accept you as Lord and Savior over my life; in Jesus's name, Amen.

Weekly Class Activities Agenda

(RECOMMENDED TIME: 1 HOUR):

- Attendance (2 minutes)
- Good News (2 minutes)
- Beginning Prayer (2 minutes)
- Discuss Virtual Class Norms (2 minutes)
- Panel Introduction (2 minutes)
- Song Video ("Imagine" by John Lennon) (Video Time 3:08)
- Discussion Topic Question(s) (20 minutes)
- Class Discussion Question(s) or Self-Reflection Question (email) (10 minutes)
- Plan of Salvation (5 minutes)
- Ending Prayer (2 minutes)
- Class Evaluation (Google Form) (10 minutes)
- Affirmations (3 minutes)

How to Teach?

The teacher will follow the Weekly Class Activities Agenda.

Beginning Prayer

Dear God bless this day that you have made and help us to rejoice and be glad in it. Give us clarity of mind, revelation of who you are, wisdom, knowledge, and discernment on how to apply each lesson to our life. Guide and direct our footsteps and show us your will and purpose for our life. Thank you for blessing us so that we may be a blessing to others. In Jesus name, Amen.

Week 21

Peace

Peace is a state of tranquility or quietness.

Select the best example for the topic of peace:

1. Julianne completed her homework and lies down on the bed with her eyes closed for twenty minutes. She is only focusing on positive thoughts and doing her breathing exercises to destress. The timer goes off, and Juliane goes downstairs for dinner.
2. Manju loves to listen to rock and roll music while working on homework assignments. The next day, she receives her grade and has another C. Manju tells her mother that she does not understand why she is only getting a C on her homework assignments. She is studying every night with her Van Halen rock music. Her mother suggests that she listen to classical music. Manju responds, "That would hurt my vibe."

Answer: 1

Purpose: This lesson aims to provide the students with skills on how to acquire and maintain peace.

Key Terms: tranquility, acquire, chaos.

Discussion Topic Question: Can you have chaos surrounding you and still have peace?

Instruction: Provide thirty seconds of wait time for the girls to respond to the question. If no one answers, then the panel and/or coordinator will respond to the question.

Answer:

If we can quiet our inner chaos, our outward stress will lessen. Peace does not mean the absence of problems, but it does mean you can live in peace amid difficulties. There can be a storm brewing up around you on the outside, but you have peace inside because you know when you trust God with the circumstance, He will give you perfect peace when you trust in Him. God is the ultimate peacemaker.

"When you feel as though you're surrounded, you have to come back to the place of peace." (Joel Osteen, p.211)

Play Youtube.com Video ("Imagine" by John Lennon, 3 minutes 8 seconds)

What does the Bible say about "peace?"

Scriptures:

A. You keep him in perfect peace whose mind is stayed on you. (Isaiah 26:3) (ESV)
B. If possible, so far as it depends on you, live peaceably with all men. (Romans 12:18) (ESV)
C. Be anxious for nothing, but in everything by prayer and supplication, with thanksgiving, let your requests be made known to God, and the peace of God, which surpasses all understanding, will guard your hearts and minds through Christ Jesus. (Philippians 4:7) (NKJV)

Self-Reflection: How can you live, maintain, or acquire more peace?

Ending Prayer/Prayer of Salvation:

Prayer of Salvation:

Dear Jesus, please forgive me for all my sins. I believe you died on the Cross and rose again. Come into my life and help me trust and follow you. I accept you as Lord and Savior over my life; in Jesus's name, Amen.

Weekly Class Activities Agenda

(RECOMMENDED TIME: 1 HOUR):

- Attendance (2 minutes)
- Good News (2 minutes)
- Beginning Prayer (2 minutes)
- Discuss Virtual Class Norms (2 minutes)
- Panel Introduction (2 minutes)
- Discussion Topic Question(s) (20 minutes)
- Class Discussion Question(s) or Self-Reflection Question (email) (10 minutes)
- Plan of Salvation (5 minutes)
- Ending Prayer (2 minutes)
- Class Evaluation (Google Form) (10 minutes)
- Affirmations (3 minutes)

How to Teach?

The teacher will follow the Weekly Class Activities Agenda.

Beginning Prayer

Dear God bless this day that you have made and help us to rejoice and be glad in it. Give us clarity of mind, revelation of who you are, wisdom, knowledge, and discernment on how to apply each lesson to our life. Guide and direct our footsteps and show us your will and purpose for our life. Thank you for blessing us so that we may be a blessing to others. In Jesus name, Amen.

Purpose: This lesson aims to help the girls have or maintain a more positive attitude toward themselves and/or life.

Key Terms: commendable, conceit, humility, humongous, imply, rivalry.

Week 22

Attitude/Behavior

Attitude/behavior is a settled way of thinking, feeling about someone or something, point of view, a position of the body, an action or a mental state.

Select the best example of a negative attitude:

1. North was not selected as a cheerleader during the school try-outs this year. She told the cheer coach that she would attend Cheer Summer School and try out again next year.
2. Reign was standing in the line for ice cream sandwiches at school when she reached the front of the line, and the school volunteer told her that they were out of desserts. Reign demanded that the school volunteer look again in the freezer. The school volunteer told her again that she was sorry, but they did not have any more of it. Reign started screaming at the volunteer and telling her that she had been standing in line for five minutes and was looking forward to the ice cream sandwich.

Answer: 2

Discussion Topic Question: What or who determines how you behave?

Instruction: Provide thirty seconds of wait time for the girls to respond to the question. If no one answers, then the panel and/or coordinator will respond to the question.

Answer:

One of the things that may determine an attitude is how a teen feels about a topic or self. Family dynamics, pressures from school, and social media can affect a teen's attitude and behavior. What type of school the teen attends can also affect their behaviors.

School is usually the first-time kids learn how to communicate and interact with their peers not unless they have a twin at home or other siblings that are older.

The kind of school environment that your child is placed in plays an enormous role in performing or acting. Some teens accept and adopt the behaviors and opinions of their friends. During this stage in life, friends become an essential part of who they are and how they navigate through the teen years.

What does the Bible say about "behavior?"

Scriptures:

A. Finally, brothers, whatever is true, whatever is honorable, whatever is just, whatever is pure, whatever is lovely, whatever is commendable, if there is any excellence, if there is anything worthy of praise, think about these things. (Philippians 4:8) (ESV)

B. Be imitators of me, as I am of Christ. (1 Corinthians 11:1–34) (ESV)

C. A Joyful heart is a good medicine, but a crushed spirit dries up the bones. (Proverbs 17:22) (ESV)

D. Do all things without grumbling and/or questioning. (Philippians 2:14) (ESV)

E. Let nothing be done through strife or vain glory; but in lowliness of mind let each esteem others better than themselves. Look not every man on his own things, but every man also on the things of others. Let this mind be in you, which was also in Christ Jesus. (Philippians 2:3-5 KJV) (ESV)

Ending Prayer/Prayer of Salvation:

Prayer of Salvation:

Dear Jesus, please forgive me for all my sins. I believe you died on the Cross and rose again. Come into my life and help me trust and follow you. I accept you as Lord and Savior over my life; in Jesus's name, Amen.

Weekly Class Activities Agenda

(RECOMMENDED TIME: 1 HOUR):

- Attendance (2 minutes)
- Good News (2 minutes)
- Beginning Prayer (2 minutes)
- Panel Introduction (2 minutes)
- Role-Playing Skit (optional) (5 minutes)
- Discussion Topic Question(s) (20 minutes)
- Class Discussion Question(s) (5 minutes)
- Plan of Salvation (5 minutes)
- Ending Prayer (2 minutes)
- Class Evaluation (Google Form) (10 minutes)
- Affirmations (3 minutes)
- **How to Teach?**
  The teacher will follow the Weekly Class Activities Agenda.

Beginning Prayer

Dear God bless this day that you have made and help us to rejoice and be glad in it. Give us clarity of mind, revelation of who you are, wisdom, knowledge, and discernment on how to apply each lesson to our life. Guide and direct our footsteps and show us your will and purpose for our life. Thank you for blessing us so that we may be a blessing to others. In Jesus name, Amen.

Purpose: This lesson aims to help students navigate through peer pressure by giving them the skills to solve problems.

Key Terms: peer, transformed, servant, deceived.

Week 23

Peer Pressure

Peer Pressure is the influence from the members of one's peer group.

Select the best example of peer pressure:

1. Sudan was changing clothes in the girls' locker room when China and Italia approached her to share a cigarette. Sudan told them that she had a cold. China asked, "What does that have to do with smoking a cigarette?" Sudan took a puff and then ran to class so that she would not be late again.
2. Candy was waiting to shower in the girls' locker room when Tulip approached her and asked, "Do you have a lighter?" Candy said, "No," Tulip said, "Ask Charlotte for a lighter." Candy told them later because she did not want to be late for class.

Answer: 1

Discussion Topic Questions: How do you handle peer pressure? Think of a time when you experienced peer pressure? List some examples of peer pressure.

Answer:

Peer pressure is a real issue that affects almost all teenagers at one point in their life.

Some of the strategies that can be used are:

1. Have the confidence to walk away.
2. Set limits and boundaries and just say No.
3. Tell the person who is pressuring you how it makes you feel.
4. Talk to a trusted adult, counselor, teacher, or principal about what you're experiencing.

5. Pray and ask God for guidance and direction on how to handle the situation.
6. Steers clear of individuals that make you feel uncomfortable.

What does the Bible say about "peer pressure?"

Scriptures:

A. Do not be conformed to this world, but be transformed by the renewal of your mind, that by testing you may discern what is the will of God, what is good and acceptable and perfect. (Romans 12:2) (ESV)
B. Do not be deceived: "Bad company ruins good morals." Wake up from your drunken stupor, as is right, and do not go on sinning. For some who do not know God, I say this is to your shame. (1 Corinthians 15:33–34) (ESV)
C. Whoever walks with the wise becomes wise, but the companion of fools will suffer harm. (Proverbs 13:20) (ESV)
D. For am I now seeking the approval of man or of God? Or am I trying to please man? If I were still trying to please man, I would not be a servant of Christ. (Galatians 1:10) (ESV)

Ending Prayer/Prayer of Salvation:

Prayer of Salvation:

Dear Jesus, please forgive me for all my sins. I believe you died on the Cross and rose again. Come into my life and help me trust and follow you. I accept you as Lord and Savior over my life; in Jesus's name, Amen.

Weekly Class Activities Agenda

(RECOMMENDED TIME: 1 HOUR):

- Attendance (2 minutes)
- Good News (2 minutes)
- Beginning Prayer (2 minutes)
- Discuss Virtual Class Norms (2 minutes)
- Panel Introduction (2 minutes)
- Play Video for Relaxation (Under Pressure Mindfulness for Teens) (Video Time 7:01)
- Discussion Topic Question(s) (20 minutes)
- Class Discussion Question(s) or Self-Reflection Question (email) (10 minutes)
- Plan of Salvation (5 minutes)
- Ending Prayer (2 minutes)
- Class Evaluation (Google Form) (10 minutes)
- Affirmations (3 minutes)

How to Teach?

The teacher will follow the Weekly Class Activities Agenda.

Beginning Prayer

Dear God bless this day that you have made and help us to rejoice and be glad in it. Give us clarity of mind, revelation of who you are, wisdom, knowledge, and discernment on how to apply each lesson to our life. Guide and direct our footsteps and show us your will and purpose for our life. Thank you for blessing us so that we may be a blessing to others. In Jesus name, Amen.

Purpose: This lesson aims to help the girls identify the symptoms of stress and teach them how to cope or manage it.

Key Terms: Cope, factor, neglect, procrastination, stress, symptom

Week 24

Stress

Stress is the body's reaction to any change that requires an adjustment or response.

Select the best example of stress:

1. Caitlyn arrived at Algebra class during her snack time to finish studying for the exam that was scheduled for that day. She opened her math notebook, only to discover that her notes were missing. She remembered that earlier the math notebook had fallen on the floor in English class, and all the paperwork had scattered. Elena, who is in her algebra class, bent over to assist with picking up the paperwork. Elena shoved some of the papers in the back of her own notebook and proceeded to the back of the room. Caitlyn approached Elena when she arrived in the math class. Caitlyn appeared to be nervous, her lips were trembling, and her tone of voice was very low and raspy as she asked Elena for the missing paperwork.
2. Barbara lost her school ID and was not able to ride the school bus home. She told her friends that she would walk home. They told her to wait and then began to walk home with her.

Answer: 1

Discussion Topic Questions: Why is it essential to be able to manage stress? How do you handle stress?

Instruction: Provide thirty seconds of wait time for the girls to respond to the question. If no one answers, then the panel and/or coordinator will respond to the question for discussion.

Answer:

It is crucial to manage stress so that you do not end up with physical or mental health problems. Managing stress also provides you the coping skills for whenever you encounter everyday life problems. Some of the ways that I manage stress are listening to chamber or classical music, exercising, meditation, remaining calm, journaling my feelings, talking to a friend, talking to a psychologist or therapist, praying, and/or reading Bible scriptures on peace.

"As kids transition from grade school to middle school, they also move from schools full of friend groups into more alien settings among kids they might know." (Donna Jackson, p.39) According to Donna Jackson another reason that can cause stress in a child's life is the shifting trend in education, which has imposed more mature expectations, behaviors, and accomplishments on children at younger ages also bring on more stress. Middle school has emerged as the new high school, as the pressure continues early on for the child to think about what colleges will they be applying to and or attending. In kindergarten all students had to be concerned about was play time. Now they have to be concerned about Standardized Testing, active-shooter drills, , budget cuts, and COVID-19 have brought on more stress. They no longer are focused on playtime, recess, a leisurely lunchtime with peers, P.E. class, dance, art and music.

Play the "Under Pressure Mindfulness for Teens" video (www.2bpresent.com)

What does the Bible say about stress?

Scriptures:

A. Do not be anxious about anything, but in everything by prayer and supplication with thanksgiving let your requests be made known to God. (Philippians 4:6) (ESV)

B. Peace, I leave with you, my peace I give to you. Not as the world gives do I give to you. Let not your hearts be troubled, neither let them be afraid. (John 14:27) (ESV)

C. Cast your burden on the Lord, and He will sustain you; He will never permit the righteous to be moved. (Psalms 55:22) (ESV)

D. Anxiety in a man's heart weighs it down but a good make it glad. (Proverbs 12:25) (ESV)

E. Therefore, do not be anxious about tomorrow, for tomorrow will be anxious for itself. Sufficient for the day is its trouble. (Matthew 6:34) (ESV)

These are some of the guidelines that the American Psychological Association uses to recognize stress in teenagers (2013) and Generation Z (2018):14

- **Irritability and anger:** Children don't always have the words to describe how they feel, and sometimes tension bubbles over into a bad mood. Stressed-out kids and teens might be more short-tempered or argumentative than average.
- **Changes in behavior:** A young child who used to be a great listener is suddenly acting out. A once-active teen now doesn't want to leave the house. Sudden changes can be a sign that stress levels are high.
- **Trouble sleeping:** A child or teen might complain of feeling tired all the time, sleep more than usual, or have trouble falling asleep at night.
- **Neglecting responsibilities:** If an adolescent suddenly drops the ball on homework, forgets obligations, or starts procrastinating more than usual, stress might be a factor.
- **Eating changes:** Eating too much or too little can both be reactions to stress.
- **Getting sick more often:** Stress often shows up as physical symptoms. Children who feel stress often report headaches or stomach aches and might make frequent trips to the school nurse's office.

How to Cope with Stress?

- **Sleep well.** Sleep is essential for physical and emotional well-being. Experts recommend nine to twelve hours of sleep a night for six- to twelve-year olds. Teens need eight to ten hours a night. Sleep needs to be a priority to keep stress in check. To protect shut-eye, limit screen use at night, and avoid keeping digital devices in the bedroom.
- **Exercise.** Physical activity is an essential stress reliever for people of all ages. The US Department of Health and Human Services recommends at least sixty minutes a day of activity for children ages six to seventeen.
- **Talk it out.** Talking about stressful situations with a trusted adult can help kids and teens put things into perspective and find solutions.
- **Make time for fun and quiet.** Just like adults, kids and teens need time to do what brings them joy, whether that's unstructured time to play with building bricks or uninterrupted hours to practice music or art. Also, while some children thrive on bouncing from one activity to the next, others need more downtime. Find a healthy balance between favorite activities and free time (American Psychological Association, 2013) and (American Psychological Association, 2018)

Ending Prayer/Prayer of Salvation:

Prayer of Salvation:

Dear Jesus, please forgive me for all my sins. I believe you died on the Cross and rose again. Come into my life and help me to trust and follow you. I accept you as Lord and Savior over my life; in Jesus's name, Amen.

Weekly Class Evaluation

(MAKE COPIES)

Name:______________________________________Date:_______________

Age:________Grade:____________Do you attend church?_________

Church Name:______________________________________

Week Number and Discussion Topic:______________________________________

Contact Phone Number:___________________________

Parent/Guardian Name:____

1. What did you learn from today's topic?
2. How will you apply what you learned today in your life?
3. Are there any other topics you would like to discuss?

Comments:

Attachments

- – Weekly Class Evaluation
- – Bible Scriptures
- – Curriculum Lessons' Key Terms
- – Lesson Activities
- – Short Scenarios
- – YouTube Videos and Lessons – Suggestions:
    - Kierra Sheard – Flaws (With Lyrics) – YouTube (Week 1: Self-Esteem)
    - India Arie – I Am Not My Hair (With Lyrics) (Week 2: Self-Worth)
    - India Arie – Video (Official Video) (Week 3: Self-Acceptance)
    - Whitney Houston/Celine Dion – The Greatest Love of All (Week 4: Love)
    - Carrie Underwood – The Champion, ft. Ludacris (Week 6: Self-Integrity)
    - Wiz Khalifa – See You Again, ft. Charlie Puth (Official Video) Furious 7 Soundtrack (Week 7: Friendships)
    - Tori Kelly – Don't You Worry 'Bout A Thing (Official Video) (Week 8: Individuality)
    - Demi Lovato – Lovely Day (Week 10: Depression)
    - Pharrell – Happy (Week 12: Attitude)
    - Katy Perry – Roar (Official) (Week 13: Insecurity)
    - Kari Jobe – No Fear (Live) (Week 15: Fear)
    - Kierra Sheard – Always Win (With Lyrics) (Week 16: Faith)
    - Take 6 – Spread Love | Live Studio Session (Week 17: Love)

- Andrea Bocelli and Céline Dion – The Prayer (Week 19: Prayer)
- Lecrae – I'll Find You, ft. Tori Kelly (Official Music Video) (Week 20: Obedience)
- John Lennon – Imagine (Week 21: Peace)
- Under Pressure Mindfulness for Teens (Week 24: Stress)
- www.2bpresent.com (7:01 minutes)

Appendix A: Key Terms

(MAKE A COPY FOR ALL STUDENTS)

WEEK 1: KEY TERMS

Adorn (noun): to make more beautiful or attractive

Apparel (noun): clothing

Discernment (noun): the ability to obtain sharp perceptions or not judge well

Entourage (noun): a group of people surrounding an important person

False Metric (noun): what a person or society uses to judge one's value or success

Narrative (noun): a spoken or written account of connected events; a story

Renew (verb): to take up again. To be renovated by an inward reformation

Stature (noun): a person's size, importance, or reputation

WEEK 2: KEY TERMS

Inward (adjective): directed toward the inside of something or someone and focused internally

Sinner (noun): a person who sins. Wrongdoer

WEEK 3: KEY TERMS

Faith (noun): complete trust or confidence in someone or something. Assurance of things hoped for, the conviction of things not seen

Grace (noun): unmerited mercy or favor that God gave to humanity by sending his son, Jesus Christ, to die on the Cross

WEEK 4: KEY TERMS

Cherish (verb): to hold something dear

Nourish (verb): keep (a feeling or a belief) in one's mind, typically for a long time

Workmanship (noun): the degree of skill with which a product has been made or a job well done

WEEK 5: KEY TERMS

Belief (noun): trust, faith that a statement is true or that something exists

Dignity (noun): the state or quality of being worthy of honor or respect

Glorify (verb): praise, worship, and by bestowing honor

WEEK 6: KEY TERMS

Ethics (noun): moral principles that govern a person's behavior

Integrity (noun): the quality of being honest and having strong moral principles

Moral (adjective): concerned with principles that are right or wrong

Secure (adjective): to make something safe by guarding or protecting it

Treacherous (adjective): guilty of or involving betrayal or deception

WEEK 7: KEY TERMS

Gracious (adjective): attitude, kind and pleasant

Loyal (noun): giving or showing firm and constant support or allegiance to a person

Quality (noun): a distinctive attribute or characteristic possessed by someone or something

Rejection (noun): the dismissing or refusal of a proposal, idea, etc.

Seasoned (adjective): a person who has been around forever, doing what they do, and doing it well

Wrathful (adjective): filled with wrath, irate, and/or anger

WEEK 8: KEY TERMS

Adorn (verb): make more beautiful or attractive

Apparel (noun): clothing

Discernment (noun): is the ability to obtain sharp perceptions or to judge well

Entourage (noun): a group of people surrounding an important person

False metric (noun): what a person or society uses to judge one's value or success

Narrative (noun): a spoken or written account of connected events; a story

Renew (verb): to take up again. To be renovated by an inward reformation

Stature (noun): a person's size, importance, or reputation

WEEK 9: KEY TERMS

Abstain (verb): restrain oneself from doing or enjoying something

Captive (noun): the state of being held, imprisoned, enslaved, or confined

Deceit (noun): the action or practice of deceiving someone by concealing or misrepresenting the truth

Moral (adjective): concerned with the principles of right and wrong behavior and the goodness or badness of human character

Philosophy (noun): the study of the fundamental nature of knowledge, reality, and existence

WEEK 10: KEY TERMS

Anxiety (noun): a feeling of worry, nervousness, or uneasiness, typically about an imminent event or something with an uncertain outcome

Depression (noun): a mood disorder that causes a persistent feeling of sadness and loss of interest

Dismayed (verb): to cause to lose courage or resolution

WEEK 11: KEY TERMS

Enhance (verb): intensify, increase, or further improve the quality or value

Holy Spirit (noun): in Christianity, the third person of the trinity

Mental health (noun): mental health includes our emotional, psychological, and social well-being. It affects how we think, feel, and act

Temple (noun): a building devoted to worship or a person's body is their holy temple.

Vigorous (adjective): strong, healthy, and full of energy

WEEK 12: KEY TERMS

Attitude (noun): a way of thinking or feeling about someone or something, typically one that's reflected in one's behavior

Gratitude (noun): the quality of being thankful, readiness to show appreciation

Thermometer (noun): an instrument for measuring and indicating temperature, a sealed glass tube

Thermostat (noun): a device that regulates temperature or that activates a device when the temperature reaches a certain point

WEEK 13: KEY TERMS

Cast (verb): to give a worry, burden, doubt, or problem to the Lord when you are praying for Him to resolve or solve it

Insecurity (noun): is a feeling of uncertainty, a lack of confidence, or anxiety about yourself

Supplication (noun): to plead humbly, a religious prayer

Thanksgiving (noun): the act of giving thanks, grateful acknowledgment of benefits or favors, especially to God

WEEK 14: KEY TERMS

Accountability (noun): the fact or condition of being accountable, responsible.

Consequence (noun): a result of an action, whether good or bad

Heartily (adverb): thoroughly or vigorously, to eat heartily

Responsibility (noun): to do something on your own without being told, being accountable

WEEK 15: KEY TERMS

Anxiety (noun): a feeling of worry, nervousness, or uneasiness

Dismayed (noun): to cause to lose courage or resolution due to alarm or fear

Righteousness (noun): free from guilt or sin, acting in accord with divine or moral law

WEEK 16: KEY TERMS

Evidence (noun): proof, confirmation, verification

Faith (noun): the assurance that the things revealed and promised in the Word are true, even though unseen, and gives the believer a conviction that what he expects in faith will come to pass

Substance (noun): the gist or main idea of something

WEEK 17: KEY TERMS

Abide (verb): to remain stable or fixed in a state, to continue in place, to conform or abide by the rules

Affirmation (noun): emotional support or encouragement

Begotten (beget) (verb): to bring a child into existence by the process of reproduction

Eternal (adjective): lasting or existing forever, without end or beginning

Perish (verb): suffer death, typically in a violent, sudden, or untimely way

Qualities (noun): features or characteristics of a person or thing

WEEK 18: KEY TERMS

Affect (verb): make a difference

Community (noun): a group of people living in the same place, feeling of fellowship with others

Exposure (noun): the state of being exposed, the revelation of an identity or fact

Harmony (noun): the playing of musical tones together in chords

Mellow (adjective): pleasantly smooth or soft, free from harshness

Perception (noun): the ability to see, hear, or become aware of something through the senses

WEEK 19: KEY TERMS

Circumstance (noun): a fact or condition connected with or relevant to an event or action.

Spiritual (adjective): relating to a religion or religious belief

WEEK 20: KEY TERMS

Authority (noun): the power or right to give orders, make decisions, and enforce obedience

Compliance (noun): the act or process of complying to a demand, desire, or proposal

Guidance (noun): advice or information aimed at resolving a problem or difficulty, especially as given by someone in authority

Obedience (noun): compliance with an order, request, or law of submission to another's authority

WEEK 21: KEY TERMS

Acquire (verb): buy or obtain

Chaos (noun): complete disorder and confusion

Tranquility (noun): the quality or state of being tranquil or calm

WEEK 22: KEY TERMS

Commendable (adjective): worthy of the highest praise

Conceit (noun): excessive pride in oneself

Humility (noun): a modest or low view of one's own importance; humbleness

Humongous (adjective): huge: enormous

Imply (verb): strongly suggest the truth or existence of something not expressly stated

Rivalry (noun): competition for the same objective or for superiority in the same field

WEEK 23: KEY TERMS

Deceive (verb): fail to admit to oneself that something is not valid

Peer (verb): one that is equal standing with another; equal

Servant (noun): a devoted and helpful follower or supporter

Transform (verb): make a thorough or dramatic change in the form, appearance, or character

WEEK 24: KEY TERMS

Cope (verb): to deal with and attempt to overcome problems and difficulties

Factor (noun): a circumstance, fact, or influence that contributes to a result or outcome

Neglect (verb): fail to care for properly

Procrastination (noun): the action of delaying or postponing something

Stress (noun): the body's reaction to any change that requires an adjustment or response

Symptom (noun): a physical or mental feature that is regarded as indicating a disease condition

Teen Curriculum

(STUDENT COPY ONLY)

Lesson 1:

Purpose: This lesson aims to increase the girls' self-esteem by reminding them that they are fearfully and wonderfully made by God and created in His image.

Key Terms: discernment, entourage, stature, false metric narrative, adorn, apparel, renewing.

Week 1: Self-Esteem, Body Image, and Dress Code

Discussion Topic Questions:

Why is having self-esteem important?

Where do I get my self-esteem from, and how can I have positive self-esteem?

What does the Bible say about "self-esteem," "body image," and "dress code?"

Scriptures:

A. You are fearfully and wonderfully made. (Psalms 139:13–14) (ESV)

B. You are altogether beautiful, my love; there is no flaw in you. (Song of Solomon 4:7) (ESV)

C. But the Lord said to Samuel, do not look on his appearance or the height of his stature because I have rejected him. The Lord sees not as man sees; man looks on the outward appearance, but the Lord looks on the heart. (1 Samuel 16:7) (ESV)

D. Do not be transformed to this world but be ye transformed by the renewing of your mind. (Romans 12:2) (ESV)

Dress Code: Dress Code is a style of dress that a person has adopted to express who they are from the outside.

Discussion Questions: How do you decide what clothing to wear in public or to school? What is acceptable and appropriate clothing for your age?

Scriptures:

A. Likewise, also that women should adorn themselves in respectable apparel, with modesty and self-control, not with braided hair and gold or pearls or costly attire. (1 Timothy 2:9) (ESV)

B. Or do you not know that your body is a temple of the Holy Spirit within you, whom you have from God. (1 Corinthians 6:19–20) (ESV)

Lesson 1: Key Terms

– Adorn (noun): to make more beautiful or attractive

– Apparel (noun): clothing

– Discernment (noun): the ability to obtain sharp perceptions or to judge well

– Entourage (noun): a group of people surrounding an important person

– False metric (noun): what a person or society uses to judge one's value or success

– Narrative (noun): a spoken or written account of connected events; a story

– Renew (verb): to take up again. To be renovated by an inward reformation

– Stature (noun): a person's size, importance, or reputation

Lesson 2:

Purpose: This lesson aims to teach and discuss why it is crucial to develop a positive self-worth.

Key Terms: sinners, inward

Week 2: Self-Worth/ Emotions/Feelings

Self-worth is how you value yourself. You are a good person and would like to be treated with respect.

Discussion Topic Question:

How do you measure or determine your self-worth?

What does the Bible say about "self-worth?"

Scriptures:

A. For you formed my inward parts: you knitted me together in my mother's womb. (Psalms 139:13–14) ESV)
B. But God shows his love for us in that while we were still sinners, Christ died for us. (Romans 5:8) (ESV)

C. How precious also are thy thoughts unto me, O God: How great is the sum of them! If I should count them, they are more in number than the sand. When I awake, I am still with thee. (Psalms 139:17–18) (KJV)

D. For I know the thoughts that I think towards you, saith the Lord, thoughts of peace, and not of evil, to give you an expected end. (Jeremiah 29:11) (KJV)

E. And we know that all things work together for good to them that love God, to them who are called according to His purpose. (Romans 8:28) (KJV)

Lesson 2: Key Terms

- Inward (adjective): directed toward the inside of something or someone and focused internally
- Sinner (noun): a person who sins; wrong doer

Lesson 3:

Purpose: This lesson aims to help girls accept their good parts, flaws, and failures.

Key Terms: faith, grace

Week 3: Self-Acceptance

Self-acceptance is acceptance of one's strengths and weaknesses: what do I like/what don't I like.

For by grace, you have been saved through faith. And this is not your own doing; it is the gift of God. (Ephesians 2:8)

Discussion Topic Questions:

Who am I? I am a child of God, and I was bought with a price.

What self-talk are you doing to encourage yourself?

What do I not like about myself?

What does the Bible say about "self-acceptance?"

Scripture:

A. For by grace, you have been saved through faith. And this is not your own doing; it is the gift of God. (Ephesians 2:8) (ESV)

Activities:

List five of your positive qualities on a sheet of paper.

List three things that you wish you could change about yourself.

List the beliefs that you learned about yourself from those close to you when you were young, such as mother, father, siblings, teachers, classmates, etc. What message do you focus on today? What do you believe about yourself, and what beliefs detract from your confidence and happiness? Are these messages or opinions accurate or something that you think is true? Which statements do you want to change that will help your self-esteem? What new thoughts would help support your beliefs and your self-esteem?

What personal characteristics or qualities do you have and admire?

Lesson 3: Key Terms

- Faith (noun): complete trust or confidence in someone or something. Assurance of things hoped for, the conviction of things not seen
- Grace (noun): unmerited mercy (favor) that God gave to humanity by sending his Son, Jesus Christ, to die on the Cross

Lesson 4:

Purpose: This lesson aims to teach the girls how to love themselves first and love others.

Key Terms: nourishes, cherishes, workmanship.

Week 4: Self-Love

Self-love is loving yourself and taking care of your needs and happiness.

Discussion Topic Questions:

What is self-love?

Why is it important to love yourself? List three reasons.

What does the Bible say about "self-love?"

Scriptures:

A. I praise you, for I am fearfully and wonderfully made. (Psalms 139:13–14) (ESV)

B. For no one ever hated his flesh but nourishes and cherishes it. (Ephesians 5:29) (ESV)

C. And above all, this put-on love, which binds everything together in perfect harmony. (Colossians 3:14) (ESV)

D. Before I formed you in the womb, I knew you before you were born. (Jeremiah 1:5) (ESV)

E. Just as He chose us in Him before the foundation before the world. (Ephesians 1:4) (ESV)

F. We are His workmanship created in Christ Jesus for good works. (Ephesians 2:10) (ESV)

Class Discussion Questions:

What are the good things that you like about yourself? What are the things you honor and appreciate about who you are? What are your strengths? What do others understand about you? Are there any good qualities that your friends possess that you wish you had? How would your friends describe you?

Read the list out loud in front of someone you trust or in front of a mirror. Recite the items you like about yourself to paint a picture and help you hear it aloud and believe it.

Example: I love my confidence. I love that I know how to be a friend. I love my ability to be respectful.

Celebrate your strengths. Call those things that are not as if they were. Say the things that God says about you.

The beforehand is before the foundation of the world. Just like God knew, He specifically prepared His plan for you and all you must do is walk in it and you will not fail. God already has mapped out His plan for your life, just as it says in Jeremiah 29:11 (ESV): "For I know the plans I have for you, declares the Lord, plans for welfare and not for evil to give you a future and a hope." It's already done; nothing can stop your destiny. Did you know that you were chosen before the foundation of the world? God knew you before you ever existed. You are not an accident. God determined our end from the beginning. He already has your life worked out for you; all you must do is just walk in it.

Lesson 4: Key Terms

– Cherish (verb): to hold something dear

– Nourish (verb): keep a feeling or a belief in one's mind, typically for a long time

– Workmanship (noun): the degree of skill with which a product is made or a job done

Lesson 5:

Purpose: This lesson aims to help girls increase their confidence and behave with grace, honor, and dignity.

Key Terms: value, belief, dignity, glorify.

Week 5: Self-Respect

Pride and confidence in oneself, a feeling that one is behaving with honor and dignity.

Discussion Topic Questions:

What is self-respect? How can you earn the respect of others?

Self-Reflection:

Who do you respect and why? What can you learn from the people you respect?

What does the Bible say about "self-respect?"

Scriptures:

A. You were bought with a price. So, glorify God in your body. (1 Corinthians 6:20)(ESV)

B. Do your best to present yourself to God as one approved, a worker who has no need to be ashamed. (2 Timothy 2:15) (ESV)

C. For we are his workmanship, created in Christ Jesus, for good works, which God prepared beforehand. (Ephesians 2:10) (ESV)

Lesson 5: Key Terms

– Belief (noun): trust, faith that a statement is true or that something exists

– Dignity (noun): the state or quality of being worthy of honor or respect

– Glorify (verb): praise, worship, and by bestowing honor

Lesson 6:

Purpose: The purpose of this lesson is to develop integrity through having solid morals and principles.

Key Terms: integrity, moral, ethics, secure, treacherous

Week 6: Self-Integrity

Self-integrity is being honest and having strong morals and principles.

Discussion Topic Question:

How do you develop self-integrity?

What does the Bible say about "self-integrity?"

Scriptures:

A. Whoever walks in integrity walks securely, but he who makes his ways crooked will be found out. (Proverbs 10:9) ESV)

B. Better is a poor man who walks in his integrity than a rich man who is crooked in his ways. (Proverbs 28:6) (ESV)

C. The integrity of the upright guides them, but the crookedness of the treacherous destroys them. (Proverbs 11:3) ESV)

Lesson 6: Key Terms

- Ethics (noun): moral principles that govern a person's behavior
- Integrity (noun): the quality of being honest and having strong moral principles
- Moral (adjective): concerned with principles that are right or wrong
- Secure (adjective): to relieve from exposure to danger: act to make safe against adverse contingencies.
- Treacherous (adjective): guilty of or involving betrayal or deception

Lesson 7:

Purpose: This lesson aims to define the qualities that make a good or loyal friend.

Key Terms: qualities, loyal, gracious, seasoned, wrathful, rejection

A friendship is a close relationship or relationship with another person.

Discussion Topic Question:

What are some of the qualities that make a person a friend?

What does the Bible say about "friendships?"

Scriptures:

A. Do not be unequally yoked with unbelievers. (2 Corinthians 6:14) (ESV)

B. Let your speech always be gracious, seasoned with salt so that you may know-how ye ought to answer every man. (Colossians 4:6) (ESV)

C. A friend loves at all times, and a brother is born for adversity. (Proverbs 17:17) (ESV)

D. A man of many companions may come to ruin, but there is a friend who sticks closer than a brother. (Proverbs 18:24) (ESV)

E. Make no friendship with a man given to anger nor go with a wrathful man. (Proverbs 22:24–25) (ESV)

F. Do not be unequally yoked with unbelievers. (2 Corinthians 6:14) (ESV)

Self-Reflection:

What are some of the good qualities/characteristics that my friends exhibit?

Lesson 7: Key Terms

- Gracious (adjective): attitude, kind, pleasant
- Loyal (adjective): giving or showing firm and constant support or allegiance to a person
- Quality (noun): a distinctive attribute or characteristic possessed by someone or something
- Rejection (noun): the dismissing or refusal of a proposal, idea, etc.
- Seasoned (adjective): a person who has been around forever, doing what they do, and doing it well
- Wrathful (adjective): filled with wrath, irate, and/or anger

Lesson 8:

Purpose: The purpose of this lesson is to help you become more aware of who you are.

Key Terms: discernment, entourage, stature, false metric, narrative, adorn, apparel, renewing.

Week 8: Individuality

Individuality is quality or character that distinguishes you from another person.

Discussion Topic Questions:

How are you different or unique from your friends? What makes you an individual?

Discussion Question:

How to become a better individual?

Homework Question:

Why is it important to know that God fearfully and wonderfully makes you?

Self-Reflection:

How can I positively promote my individuality?

What does the Bible say about "individuality?"

Scriptures:

A. Why, even the hairs of your head are all numbered. Fear not you are of more value than many sparrows. (Luke 12:7) (ESV)

B. But even the hairs of your head are all numbered. (Matthew 10:30) (ESV)

C. So, God created man in His own image; in the image of God, He created him; male and female He created them. (Genesis 1:27) (ESV)

Lesson 8: Key Terms

– Adorn (verb): make more beautiful or attractive

– Apparel (noun): clothing

– Discernment (noun): the ability to obtain sharp perceptions or to judge well

– Entourage (noun): a group of people surrounding an important person

– False Metric (noun): what a person or society uses to judge one's value or success

– Narrative (noun): a spoken or written account of connected events; a story

– Renew (verb): to take up again. To be renovated by an inward reformation

– Stature (noun): a person's size, importance, or reputation

Lesson 9:

Purpose: The purpose of this lesson is to show you how to impact and influence other people's lives positively.

Key Terms: captive, philosophy, deceit, moral, abstain

Week 9: Influence

Influence is how you affect another person's character or development.

Discussion Topic Question:

How can you make a positive influence in someone's life?

What does the Bible say about being a "positive influence" on others?

Scriptures:

A. Do not be deceived: Bad company ruins good morals. (1 Corinthians 15:33) (ESV)

B. See to it that no one takes up captive by philosophy and empty deceit. (Colossians 2:8) (ESV)

C. Abstain from every form of evil. (1 Thessalonians 5:22) (ESV)

Lesson 9: Key Terms

- Abstain (verb): restrain oneself from doing or enjoying something
- Captive (noun): the state of being held, imprisoned, enslaved, or confined
- Deceit (noun): the action or practice of deceiving someone by concealing or misrepresenting the truth
- Moral (adjective): concerned with the principles of right and wrong behavior and the goodness or badness of human character
- Philosophy (noun): the study of the fundamental nature of knowledge, reality, and existence

Lesson 10:

Purpose: This lesson aims to determine if you are depressed and when you should reach out to someone for help.

Key Terms: depression, dismayed, anxiety.

Week 10: Depression

Depression is a mood disorder that causes someone to feel sad or lost. It also involves the body, mood, and thoughts that affect how a person eats, their periods of sleep, how they think about herself, and their beliefs.

Homework Question:

Who do you reach out to whenever you are depressed?

What does the Bible say about "depression?"

Bible Story Reference:

The story of Elijah running away from Ahab and Jezebel. (1 Kings 19)

Scriptures:

A. When the righteous cry for help, the Lord hears and delivers them out of all their troubles. (Psalms 34:17–18) (ESV)

B. Fear not for I am with you; be not dismayed for I am your God. (Isaiah 41:10) (ESV)

C. Casting all your anxieties on him because he cares for you. (1 Peter 5:7) (ESV)

Lesson 10: Key Terms

- Anxiety (noun): a feeling of worry, nervousness, uneasiness typically about an imminent event or something with an uncertain outcome
- Depression (noun): a mood disorder that causes a persistent feeling of sadness and loss of interest
- Dismayed (verb): to cause to lose courage or resolution

Lesson 11:

Purpose: The purpose of this lesson is to learn how exercise can benefit your body and mood.

Discussion Topic: Exercise

Key Terms: vigorously, enhances, Holy Spirit, mental health, temple.

Week 11 : Exercise

Activity requiring physical effort, carried out to maintain or improve health and fitness.

Discussion Topic Question:

Why is exercise so important for a teenager's health?

Self-Reflection:

What type of exercises are you involved in regularly? Is there anything prohibiting you from exercising? What? Do you have any health problems that prohibit you from exercising, or do you need to modify an exercise program?

What does the Bible say about "exercise?"

Scriptures:

A. For a while, bodily training is of some value; godliness is of importance in every way, as it holds promise. (1 Timothy 4:8) (ESV)

B. Or do you not know that your body is a temple of the Holy Spirit within you. (1 Corinthians 6:19–20) (ESV)

C. I can do all things through him who strengthens me. (Philippians 4:13). (ESV)

D. Stop seeing giants around you. Begin to see yourself conquering everything!

Lesson 11: Key Terms

- Enhance (verb): intensify, increase, or further improve the quality or value
- Holy Spirit (noun): in Christianity, the third person of the trinity
- Mental health (noun): mental health includes our emotional, psychological, and social well-being. It affects how we think, feel, and act
- Temple (noun): a building devoted to worship or a person's body is their holy temple
- Vigorous (noun): strong, healthy, and full of energy

Lesson 12:

Purpose: The purpose of this lesson is to show you how your attitude can affect your day.

Key Terms: attitude, gratitude, thermostat, thermometer

Week 12: Attitude

Attitude is a feeling about something or someone.

Discussion Topic Questions:

Why is it good to have a positive attitude about life? How should you begin your day if you want it to go well?

What does the Bible say about having a "positive attitude?"

Scriptures:

A. You will be above only and not beneath. You will always be at the top. (Deuteronomy 28:13) (ESV)

B. Refuse to accept any other type of thinking. Be a thermostat and not a thermometer. Set the thermostat of your attitude to "Above Only."

C. I can do all things through Jesus Christ, who strengthens me. (Philippians 4:13) (ESV)

D. Stop seeing giants around you. Start seeing the giant inside of you. Begin to see yourself conquering everything!

Lesson 12: Key Terms

- Attitude (noun): a way of thinking or feeling about someone or something, typically one that's reflected in one's behavior
- Gratitude (noun): the quality of being thankful, readiness to show appreciation
- Thermometer (noun): an instrument for measuring and indicating temperature, a sealed glass tube
- Thermostat (noun): a device that regulates temperature or that activates a device when the temperature reaches a certain point

Lesson 13:

Purpose: This lesson aims to help you become more secure and confident with who you are.

Key Terms: cast, insecurity, supplication, thanksgiving

Week 13 : Insecurity

Insecurity is the lack of confidence.

Discussion Topic Questions:

What makes you feel secure or confident about yourself? What is the one thing that you are insecure about?

What does the Bible say about "insecurity?"

Scriptures:

A. You are altogether beautiful my love, there is no flaw in you. (Song of Solomon 4:7) (ESV)

B. Do not be anxious about anything, but in everything by prayer and supplication with thanksgiving, let your requests be made known to God. (Philippians 4:6) (ESV)

C. And you will know the truth, and the truth shall set you free. (John 8:32) (ESV)

D. You will be secure because there is hope, you will look about you and take your rest in safety. You will lie down with no one to make you afraid... (Job 11:18-19) (ESV)

Self-Reflection:

Think about the things that make you feel insecure. Pray, and cast that care upon God. God does not make us feel insecure; it comes from negative things that others and the enemy have said about us.

Lesson 13: Key Terms

- Cast (verb): to give a worry, burden, doubt, or problem to the Lord when you are praying for Him to resolve or solve
- Insecurity (noun): a feeling of uncertainty, a lack of confidence or anxiety about yourself
- Supplication (noun): to plead humbly, a religious prayer
- Thanksgiving (noun): the act of giving thanks, grateful acknowledgment of benefits or favors, especially to God

Lesson 14:

Purpose: This lesson aims to teach the students why being a responsible person is essential.

Key Terms: accountability, consequences, heartily, responsibility

Week 14: Responsibility

Responsibility is the ability to do something without being told or asked. You also accept blame for your actions.

Discussion Topic Question:

Why should teens be held responsible for their actions?

Self-Reflection:

What are some responsibilities teens should have?

What does the Bible say about "responsibility?"

Scriptures:

A. For each will have to bear his load. (Galatians 6:5) (ESV)

B. Whatever you do, work heartily as for the Lord and not for men. (Colossians 3:23) (ESV)

Lesson 14: Key Terms

- Accountability (noun): the fact or condition of being accountable, responsible.
- Consequence (noun): a result of an action, whether good or bad
- Heartily (adverb): thoroughly or vigorously, to eat heartily
- Responsibility (noun): to do something on your own without being told, being accountable

Lesson 15:

Purpose: This lesson aims to teach the teens what to do with their fear(s) or anxieties.

Key Terms: anxiety, dismayed, righteousness.

Week 15: Fear

Fear is being afraid of something or someone.

Discussion Topic Question:

Is fear real?

What does the Bible say about "fear?"

Scriptures:

A. Fear not, for I am with you; be not dismayed, for I am your God. I will strengthen you. I will help you; I will uphold you with my righteous right hand. (Isaiah 41:10) (ESV)

B. For God has not given us a spirit of fear but of power, love, and a sound mind. (2 Timothy 1:7) (ESV)

C. I sought the Lord, and He answered me and delivered me from all my fears. (Psalms 34:4) (ESV)

Lesson 15: Key Terms

- Anxiety (noun): a feeling of worry, nervousness, or uneasiness
- Dismayed (noun): to cause to lose courage or resolution due to alarm or fear
- Righteousness (noun): free from guilt or sin, acting in accord with divine or moral law

Lesson 16:

Purpose: The purpose of this lesson is to teach the girls how to exercise their faith.

Key Terms: evidence, faith, substance

Week 16: Faith

Faith is the substance of things hoped for and the evidence of things not seen.

Discussion Topic Question:

What is faith?

What does the Bible say about "faith?"

Scriptures:

A. What is something that you have prayed for or asked God to do for you?

B. And whatever you ask in prayer, you will receive if you have faith. (Matthew 21:22) (ESV)

C. For we walk by faith and not by sight. (2 Corinthians 5:7) (ESV)

D. All things are possible to him who believes. (Mark 9:23) (ESV)

E. Faith is the substance of things hoped for and the evidence of things not seen. (Hebrews 11:1) (KJV)

Lesson 16: Key Terms

- Evidence (noun): proof, confirmation, verification
- Faith (noun): the assurance that the things revealed and promised in the Word are true, even though unseen, and gives the believer a conviction that what he expects in faith will come to pass
- Substance (noun): the gist or main idea of something

Lesson 17:

Purpose: The purpose of this lesson is to develop vital self-love.

Key Terms: abide, affirmation, begotten, eternal, perish, qualities.

Week 17: Love

Love is having an intense feeling for something or someone.

Discussion Topic Questions:

How or why should you love yourself? Are you able to help and love your enemies?

What does the Bible say about love?

Scriptures:

A. Love is patient and kind; love does not envy or boast; it is not arrogant or rude. (1 Corinthians 13:4–8) (ESV)

B. For God so loved the world, that He gave His only begotten Son, that whoever believes in Him should not perish but have eternal life. (John 3:16) (ESV)

C. So now faith, hope, and love abide, these three; but the greatest of these is love. (1 Corinthians 13:13) (ESV)

Lesson 17: Key Terms

- Abide (verb): to remain stable or fixed in a state, to continue in place, to conform or abide by the rules.
- Affirmation (noun): emotional support or encouragement
- Begotten (beget) (verb): to bring a child into existence by the process of reproduction.
- Eternal (adjective): lasting or existing forever, without end or beginning.
- Perish (verb): suffer death, typically in a violent, sudden, or untimely way.
- Qualities (noun): features or characteristics of a person or thing

Lesson 18:

Purpose: This lesson aims to understand how what you listen to can affect your mood and attitude.

Key Terms: affect, community, exposure, harmony, mellow, perception

Week 18: Music

Music is vocal or instrumental sounds that can be combined to produce harmony or an expression of emotion.

Discussion Topic Question:

How does the type of music you listen to affect your attitude?

What does the Bible say about "music?"

Scriptures:

A. What type of music do you listen to regularly? Do you enjoy worship music? How does music affect your self-esteem or attitude?

B. Sing to Him, sing praises to Him; tell of all His wondrous works! (Psalms 105:2) (ESV)

C. Praise the Lord, for the Lord, is good; sing to His name, for it is pleasant! (Psalms 135:3) (ESV)

Lesson 18: Key Terms

– Affect (verb): make a difference

– Community (noun): a group of people living in the same place, feeling of fellowship with others

– Exposure (noun): the state of being exposed, the revelation of an identity or fact

– Harmony (noun): the playing of musical tones together in chords

– Mellow (adjective): pleasantly smooth or soft, free from harshness

– Perception (noun): the ability to see, hear, or become aware of something through the senses

Lesson 19:

Purpose: The purpose of this lesson is to establish a closer relationship with the Lord through prayer.

Key Terms: circumstances, spiritual

Week 19: Prayer

Prayer is communication with God. Prayer moves the hand that rules the world.

Discussion Topic Questions:

What is the purpose of prayer? What can we expect when we pray? How does prayer change our life? How do we know what to pray?

What does the Bible say about "prayer?"

Scriptures:

A. Do not be anxious about anything, but in everything by prayer and supplication with thanksgiving, let your requests be made known to God. (Philippians 4:6) (ESV)

B. If you abide in me, and my words abide in you, ask whatever you wish, and it will be done for you. (John 15:7) (ESV)

Lesson 19: Key Terms

- Circumstance (noun): a fact or condition connected with or relevant to an event or action
- Spiritual (adjective): relating a religion or religious belief

Lesson 20:

Purpose: This lesson aims to understand why being obedient can give you a longer life.

Key Terms: authority, compliance, guidance, obedience

Week 20: Obedience

Obedience is being compliant with an order.

What does the Bible say about "obedience?"

Scriptures:

A. If you love me, you will keep my commandments. (John 14:15) (ESV)

B. But He said, "Blessed rather are those who hear the word of God and keep it." (Luke 11:28) (ESV)

C. Do not merely listen to the word and do deceive yourselves. Do what it says.

D. (James 1:22) (NIV)

Lesson 20: Key Terms

– Authority (noun): the power or right to give orders, make decisions, and enforce obedience

– Compliance (noun): the act or process of complying to a demand, desire, or proposal

- Guidance (noun): advice or information aimed at resolving a problem or difficulty, especially as given by someone in authority
- Obedience (noun): compliance with an order, request, or law or submission to another's authority

Lesson 21:

Purpose: This lesson aims to provide the students with skills on how to acquire and maintain peace.

Key Terms: tranquility, acquire, chaos.

Week 21: Peace

Peace is freedom from disturbance, tranquility.

Discussion Topic Question:

Can you have chaos surrounding you and live in peace?

Self-Reflection:

How can you live, maintain, or acquire more peace?

What does the Bible say about "peace?"

Scriptures:

A. God will keep you in perfect peace when your mind is stayed on Him. (Isaiah 26:3) (ESV)

B. If possible, so far as it depends on you, live peaceably with all men. (Romans 12:18) (ESV)

C. Be anxious for nothing, but in everything by prayer and supplication, with thanksgiving, let your requests be made known to God, and the peace of God, which surpasses all understanding, will guard your hearts and minds through Christ Jesus. (Philippians 4:7) (NKJV)

Lesson 21: Key Terms

– Acquire (verb): buy or obtain

– Chaos (noun): complete disorder and confusion

– Tranquility (noun): the quality or state of being tranquil or calm

Lesson 22:

Purpose: This lesson aims to help girls have or maintain a more positive attitude toward themselves and/or life.

Discussion Topic: Attitude/Behavior

Key Terms: commendable, conceit, humility, humongous, imply, rivalry

Week 22: Attitude/Behavior

A settled way of thinking or feeling about someone or something, a point of view, a position of the body proper to or implying an action or mental state.

Discussion Topic Question:

What does the Bible say about "attitude" or "behavior?"

Scriptures:

A. Finally, brothers, whatever is true, whatever is honorable, whatever is just, whatever is pure, whatever is lovely, whatever is commendable, if there is any excellence, if there is anything worthy of praise, think about these things. (Philippians 4:8) (ESV)

B. Be imitators of me, as I am of Christ. (1 Corinthians 11:1–34) (ESV)

C. A Joyful heart is a good medicine, but a crushed spirit dries up the bones. (Proverbs 17:22) (ESV)

D. Do all things without grumbling and/or questioning. (Philippians 2:14) (ESV)

E. Do nothing from rivalry or conceit, but in humility count others more significant than yourselves. Let each of you look not only to his own interests but also to the interests of others. Have this mind among yourselves, which is yours in Christ Jesus. (Philippians 2:4–5) (ESV)

Lesson 22: Key Terms:

- Commendable (adjective) admire.
- Conceit (noun) self-admiration
- Humility (noun) modesty
- Humongous (adjective) huge; enormous
- Imply (verb) inferred.
- Rivalry (noun) competition

Lesson 23:

Purpose: This lesson aims to help students navigate through peer pressure by giving them the skills to solve problems.

Key Terms: peer, transformed, servant, deceived.

Week 23: Peer Pressure

Peer pressure is the influence from the members of one's peer group.

Discussion Topic Question:

How do you handle peer pressure?

What does the Bible say about "peer pressure?"

Scriptures:

A. Do not be conformed to this world, but be transformed by the renewal of your mind, that by testing you may discern what is the will of God, what is good and acceptable and perfect. (Romans 12:2) (ESV)

B. Do not be deceived: "Bad company ruins good morals." Wake up from your drunken stupor, as is right, and do not go on sinning. For some have no knowledge of God, I say this is to your shame. (1 Corinthians 15:33–34) (ESV)

C. Whoever walks with the wise becomes wise, but the companion of fools will suffer harm. (Proverbs 13:20) (ESV)

D. For am I now seeking the approval of man or of God? Or am I trying to please man? If I were still trying to please man, I would not be a servant of Christ. (Galatians 1:10) (ESV)

Lesson 23: Key Terms:

– Peer (noun) someone at your own level.

– Transformed (verb) change.

– Servant (noun) helper.

– Deceived (verb) trick.

Lesson 24:

Purpose: This lesson aims to help the girls identify the symptoms of stress and teach them how to cope or manage it.

Key Terms: cope, factor, neglect, procrastination, stress, symptom.

Week 24: Stress

Stress is the body's reaction to any change that requires an adjustment or response.

Discussion Topic Question:

Why is it essential to be able to manage stress? How do you handle stress?

What does the Bible say about "stress?"

Scriptures:

A. Do not be anxious about anything, but in everything by prayer and supplication with thanksgiving, let your requests be made known to God. (Philippians 4:6) (ESV)

B. Peace, I leave with you, my peace I give to you. Not as the world gives do I give to you. Let not your hearts be troubled, neither let them be afraid. (John 14:27) (ESV)

C. Cast your burden on the Lord, and He will sustain you; He will never permit the righteous to be moved. (Psalms 55:22) (ESV)

D. Anxiety in a man's heart weighs him down, but a good word makes it glad. (Proverbs 12:25) (ESV)

E. Therefore, do not be anxious about tomorrow, for tomorrow will be anxious for itself sufficient for the day is its own trouble. (Matthew 6:3) (ESV)

Lesson 24: Key Terms:

- Neglect (verb) fail to care for properly.
- Procrastination (noun) the action of delaying or postponing something.
- Stress (noun) a state of mental or emotional strain or tension resulting from adverse or very demanding circumstances.
- Symptom (noun) a physical or mental feature which is regarded as indicating a condition of disease, particularly such a feature that is made apparent to the patient.

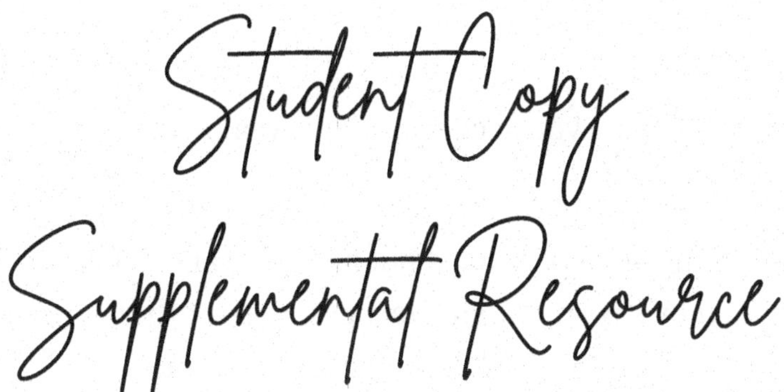

(SOCIAL STORIES FOR EACH LESSON)

Week 1

Select the best example that pertains to low self-esteem:

1. Karen, the Volleyball team captain, yells out loud in front of the entire class, "Susan please get away from me; you smell like a dirty bum." Susan becomes embarrassed and runs off the volleyball court in tears. Janessa runs after Susan to make sure she is okay.
2. Jennifer is walking to school alone when a classmate in a black car yells out the window, "Hey, lovely Jenny." Jenny ignores the classmate in the black car and continues walking to school without batting an eye.

Week 2

Select the best example that pertains to knowing your self-worth:

1. Karen is getting ready for school and is putting on her mandated school uniform that consists of a navy-blue cotton skirt and a maroon polo shirt with the school's name embroidered on the front. Karen's friends tease her for dressing like a nerd. Karen informs them that she likes looking studious at school because it makes her feel and learn like a student. She saves her other clothes for the weekends.
2. Clementine is dressing for Picture Day today at the middle school. She decides to wear cut-off jeans and a thin red-striped midriff top to show off the body piercing above her

navel area. She got the body piercing because Jeremy told her it would make her look good.

Week 3

Select the best example that shows you accepting your weaknesses:

1. In the math exam, Josephine receives a 54 percent, and Tanya gets an 86 percent. Tanya was bragging and boasting about her score and called Josephine "stupid." Josephine responded by saying, "I will start going to math tutoring with the teacher after school because I struggle with basic algebra concepts and algebraic expressions this school year.
2. Ronnie scored a 62 percent in the math exam, and Beyonce scored a 96 percent. Ronnie told Beyonce that she failed the math exam because Mr. Stafford, the math teacher, does not like her and has to fail someone to keep his job.

Week 4

Select the best example that shows you are making yourself a priority:

1. Mary is in the lunch line with some of her friends. Jane asks Mary for $3.50 to purchase lunch. Mary only has $4.50 for lunch, and she gives Jane the $3.50 because Jane says that she will pay her back tomorrow. Mary uses the $1.00 to purchase a bag of hot Cheetos with lime for her lunch.
2. Christina forgot her lunch money today and asked Joanna if she could borrow $3.50 until tomorrow. Joanna informed Christina that she only had enough money to purchase lunch for herself and that she was famished after running the mile for the physical education class today. Joanna told Christina that she could go to the front office and call home for someone to bring her the lunch money.

Week 5

Select the best example that shows a girl with self-respect:

1. Vivian was in the locker room with the other basketball team members. The team members asked Vivian to hang out with them at the bridge after school to try the new flavored Vape Pen that Amber stole from the gas station. Vivian told them that she did not want to hang out smoking with them because it is terrible for their health, and they could still get suspended if caught even though they would be off campus. One of the girls laughed and shouted, "Well, if we die, then the principal cannot suspend us."

2. Julie Ann and Adriana were texting about meeting over at Michael's house to party. His parents were away for a conference, and his older brother was in charge. There would be plenty of food, drinks, and loud music. Julie Ann texted Adriana back and gave her the directions to Michael's house and said that she would meet her there after school.

Week 6

Select the best example that shows you having integrity:

1. Darlene stole a $10 bill from her mother's purse so that she could have money to attend the movies after school. Whenever her mother mentioned that she was missing $10 from her wallet, Darlene would just keep silent and go to her bedroom.
2. Sarah was running late for school, and her dad was asleep in the bed. Sarah reached into his wallet and took out a $20 bill to pay for her school pictures. After she arrived at school, she contacted her dad on the phone to explain her actions. She told him that she would pay him back on payday. He told her to keep the money and put it in the bank for her college fund, and he thanked her for calling him.

Week 7

Select the best answer for the story that shows a friendship:

1. Maritza and Olga enjoy going to the mall to shop on Fridays. After shopping, they like attending the movies for fun. Maritza likes eating the hot buttered popcorn with peanuts, and she always orders a Slurpee and a hotdog. Olga likes red vines licorice and a hot dog with mustard. The girls are now twelve and have been friends since kindergarten.
2. Jada and Amber both go to the Lakewood Mall on Fridays after school. Jada goes with Amber but ditches her to go and hang out with her boyfriend. Amber goes with Jada so that her mother will think they are at the mall shopping together.

Week 8

Select the best example that shows being an individual:

1. Sara and Cara are twin sisters who are in the sixth grade at Chandler Middle School. Sara and Cara enjoy dressing alike and spending time together every day.
2. Stormy and Rain are twin sisters who do not look alike, nor do they like dressing alike. They both have different friends. Stormy loves chocolate ice cream, and Rain loves bubble-gum ice cream. They each have their rooms at home. When home, they like

talking and watching movies together, but they enjoy having their space when possible. Storm dyed her hair pink and purple, and Rain likes wearing her hair in red and blue dreadlocks.

Week 9

Select the best example of a person having a positive influence on someone else:

1. Myra has a six-year-old sister whom she helps get ready in the mornings before school. She fixes her sister Tyra's breakfast and makes her snack and lunch. Tyra knows that Myra loves her because Myra places a colored Post-it in her lunch box daily with a smiley face.
2. Jessie has a seven-year-old brother who loves to follow her around at home. Jessie locks him out of her room and hardly spends any time with him because she is too busy. She tells him, "Go away, you little creep."

Week 10

Select the best example that shows a girl being depressed:

1. Rachel asks Jonathan if he completed last night's homework. Jonathan tells Rachel that he does not remember the language arts teacher giving out any homework assignment. Rachel sighs and tells Jonathan, thank you.
2. Ramona is sitting in the back of the classroom, just staring into space. The teacher contacted Ramona's mother to inform her of the behavior. Ramona's mom will be coming to pick her up from school. Ramona is sorrowful because her Abuela died last night.

Week 11

Select the best example of someone exercising to increase their heart rate:

1. Catarina runs five laps on the track and field track after school five times a week to increase her endurance and maintain excellent physical fitness. On Fridays, at school, she is always energized and enthusiastic about running the mile. Catarina would like to be a personal fitness trainer for celebrities as a career.
2. Today is Friday; the students will be given a physical education test to see how fast they can run a mile. Sunny and her friends never run or jog during this time. They are socializing and looking at videos on their cellphone.

Week 12

Select the best example that shows a student displaying a negative attitude:

1. Felicia was scheduled for a science presentation today but yelled out to Mr. Rivera, "I'm not going to do the stupid project," and continued to talk with a classmate. Mr. Rivera gave her a detention slip to discuss what happened in class.
2. In front of the class, Maria gives her presentation on how she built a generator from scratch to produce electricity. The teacher and students are very impressed with the presentation. Maria would like to become an engineer after high school. All the other engineers in Maria's family are males. She will be the first female engineer in the family.

Week 13

Select the best example that shows insecurity:

1. Today is the day that Cynthia will join the nutrition and weight-loss class after school.

   The first step is that the girls must weigh themselves and put the information into the fitness tracker. Cynthia refuses to weigh herself in front of the other girls. She tells the teacher that she will complete the activity at home tonight. Cynthia does not want the other girls to know how much she weighs because they will laugh out loud and shame her or tell others at school.
2. Whenever the teacher asks for a volunteer to be weighed, North raises her hand and stands on the scale next. Shawnee is another girl who has a small built and weighs 105 pounds. She is five feet, five inches tall. She is the girl whom all the others would love to hate because she has a high metabolism and can eat anything and not gain weight. The girls do not know that North has brain cancer and exercises frequently and has to take medication daily. It is easy to judge a person by how they look instead of getting to know them.

Week 14

Select the best example that shows a girl being responsible:

1. Today is the day that Janice's mother begins working as a doctor at the hospital. Janice's dad is in bed resting because he worked four days in a row as fire chief for Los Angeles County Fire Department. Janice's responsibility is to take Jumanji, their rottweiler dog, out for a walk before she leaves for school. Janice receives a text message from

Robert, a friend, and responds to the text message. She grabs her black hoodie jacket and is out the door, leaving Jumanji in the living room without food or water to drink.

2. Cheyenne goes straight home after the cheerleading practice every day after school. She puts away her books and changes clothes. Next, Cheyenne gets a plastic bag, gloves, and a scoop so that she can walk Thunder, their massive, muscular-built bull mastiff. After walking him, she takes him to the dog park to socialize with the other dogs. Thunder always enjoys playing with the other dogs, especially Lola, the French terrier.

Week 15

Select the best example that exhibits fear:

1. When walking to school with Jenoa, Magdalena saw a strange-looking man walking toward them. She and Jenoa began to tremble while interlocking their fingers together and running across the street screaming. A few of the boys in Jenoa's math class ran to their aid, and the stranger started running in the opposite direction.
2. Victoria was lying on the bed at night when she felt the bed begin to shake. Her dad called out to her to see if she was okay. He came into her bedroom to inform her that there had been an earthquake. Victoria responded by saying, "Thanks, Dad, and have a good night."

Week 16

Select the best example of the story that shows a student exhibiting faith:

1. Nona had applied to ten law schools for enrollment within the last ten months while still in high school. She was waiting for the mail carrier to see if she had received any school acceptance letters. The mail carrier arrived and told Nona that he did not have any mail for her today. She told him, "Thank you," and went into the house to assist her mother with dinner. Nona told her mother that she had not received any mail yet but still believed that the answers were on their way.
2. Teri filled out a job application one day at Best Buy to stock their shelves during the Christmas season. She turned in the application to Bill, the manager, and asked when he would contact her about who got the job; he told her, "In three days." Teri called him for the next three days to see if he had selected someone for the position. Each time she called; he had not decided. Bill informed Teri that the decision would be made by mid-day, and he would call her at the end of the day.

Week 17

Select the best example that depicts love:

1. Lola went to the shopping mall to purchase a bracelet and earrings for her mother's birthday tomorrow. She used an application to create the birthday card with heart-shaped symbols, streamers, and the words, "Thank you, Mom, for all you have done for the family and me."
2. Tomorrow will be Sidney's little sister's birthday. Kathleen will be turning five years old. Sidney asked her mom to take her to the store to purchase a birthday present for Kathleen. When Sidney got to the shopping mall, she ditched her mom and hooked up with her friends and bought a pair of pink sparkling earrings and blouse to match for Picture Day tomorrow at school.. While the family was celebrating Kathleen's birthday, they were waiting on Sidney to present her gift. Sidney handed Kathleen a card that she had made from construction paper. Sidney's mom and the other family members looked dumbfounded. Kathleen hugged Sidney and said, "Thank you."

Week 18

Select the best example of listening to appropriate music:

1. Tamera loves to dance and sing. Her parents have taken her phone from her on numerous occasions because she likes listening to music with explicit lyrics, which are inappropriate for her age. Tamera's selection of music and friends has changed because Tamera wants to hang out with the popular and rebel students at school.
2. Lee Shan Ming loves listening to rhythm and blues music whenever she is finished with her homework. Lee sings in the choir at school and plays the keyboard for the church choir. Lee enjoys writing music and playing in the band after school.

Week 19

Select the best example of prayer:

1. Tomorrow will be the National Day of Prayer. Monica has been calling her classmates to see if they can join her outside of the flagpole to pray for the schools, communities, and country.
2. Susanne approaches Dyan at church and tells her that she is nervous about singing in the church play today and asked her if she would pray with her to have courage and confidence. Dyan ignores at Susanne and walks away.

Week 20

Select the best answer that portrays being obedient:

1. The Art teacher has warned Lori that her cellphone will be confiscated if it rings again in the classroom. Lori's cellphone rings again, and the teacher asks Lori for the cellphone.

   Lori places the phone on her desk. Lori tells the teacher that she would rather go to the front office than give her the cellphone. The teacher sends Lori to the front office. The security guard in the front office ends up confiscating Lori's phone, and she will not get it returned to her until school is over at the end of the year.

2. Tanisha is walking in line to the high school with the eighth-grade students from Triumph when her cellphone rings. The teacher asks Tanisha for the phone and informs her that she will receive it once they return to school. Tanisha gives the cellphone to the teacher.

Week 21

Select the best example for the topic of peace:

1. Julianne completed her homework and lay down on the bed with her eyes closed for twenty minutes. She is only focusing on positive thoughts and doing her breathing exercises to destress. The timer goes off, and Julianne goes downstairs for dinner.
2. Manju loves to listen to rock and roll music while working on homework assignments. The next day, she receives her grade and has another C. Manju tells her mother that she does not understand why she is only getting a C in her homework assignments. She is studying every night with her Van Halen rock music. Her mother suggests that she listen to classical music. Manju responds, "That would hurt my vibe."

Week 22

Select the best example of a negative attitude:

1. North was not selected as a cheerleader during the school try-outs this year. She told the cheerleading coach that she would attend Cheerleading Summer School and try out again next year.
2. Reign was standing in the line for ice cream sandwiches at school when she reached the front of the line, and the school volunteer told her that they were out of desserts. Reign demanded that the school volunteer look again in the freezer. The school volunteer told her again that she was sorry, but they did not have any more of it. Reign started

screaming at the volunteer and telling her that she had been standing in line for five minutes and was looking forward to the ice cream sandwich.

Week 23

Select the best example of someone experiencing peer pressure:

1. Sudan was changing clothes in the girl's locker room when China and Italia approached her to share an e-cigarette. Sudan told them that she had a cold. China asked, "What does that have to do with smoking a cigarette?" Sudan took a puff and then ran to class so that she would not be late again.
2. Candy was waiting to shower in the girls' locker room when Tulip approached her and asked, "Do you have a lighter?" Candy said, "No," and left the girls' locker room.

Week 24

Select the best example of someone experiencing stress:

1. Caitlyn arrived at algebra class during her snack time to finish studying for the exam that was scheduled that day. She opened her math notebook, only to discover that her notes were missing. She remembered that, earlier, the math notebook had fallen on the floor in the English class, and all the paperwork had scattered. Elena, who is in her algebra class, bent over to assist with picking up the paperwork. Elena shoved some of the papers in the back of her own notebook and proceeded to the back of the room. Caitlyn approached Elena when she arrived in the math class. Caitlyn appeared to be nervous, her lips were trembling, and her tone of voice was very low and raspy as she asked Elena for the missing paperwork.
2. Barbara lost her school ID and was not able to ride the school bus home. She told her friends that she would walk home. They told her to wait and then began to walk home with her.

References

American Psychology Association. Nd.

Blakes, Robert C. Jr.. 2004. The Father Daughter Talk: Untapped Potential.

Chapman, Gary and Paige Haley Drygas. 2016. A Teen's Guide To The 5 Love Languages: Northfield Publishing.

Cloud, Dr. Henry and John Townsend. 2000. Boundaries in Dating, Healthy Choices Grow Healthy Relationships: Zondervan.

Damour, Dr. Lisa. 2023. Emotional Lives of Teens: Balantine Books by Penguin Random House LLC.

Damour, Dr. Lisa 2016. Untangled: Balantine Books.

Flavin-Hall D. K., 2019, October 24. How To Help Children and Teens Manage Their Stress.

Flavin-Hall D. K. 2013. Stress in America. American Psychological Association. Daniel K.

Hall-Flavin D. K., 2018. Generation Z. American Psychological Association

Gaskins, Sheri and Tony A. Jr.. 2020. A Wonan's Influence: Howard Books.

Gerelds, Jennifer. 2018. Rest In Hope: Dayspring

Jackson, Donna. 2022. Girls On The Brink: Harmony Books and imprint of Random House.

Jones, Nona. 2020. Success From The Inside Out: Zondervan.

Meeker, Dr. Meg. 2020. Raising A Strong Daughter In A Toxic Culture: Regney Publishing.

Meyer, Joyce. 2020. Do It Afraid: Faith Group Hatchette Book Group.

Osteen, Joel. 2021. You Are Stronger Than You Think: Hatchette Book Group.

Porges, Dr. Marisa. 2020. What Girls Need, How to Raise Bold and Courageous Women:

Penguin Books.

Sophy Dr. 2022. Reset trust, Boundaries and Connections with Your Child: Simon and Schuster Inc.

Roberts, Sarah Jakes. 2017. Don't Settle For Safe: Nelson Books.

Shirer, Priscilla. 2016. Fervent: B&H Publishing Group.

Sophy Dr. 2022. Reset trust, Boundaries and Connections with Your Child: Simon and Schuster Inc.

Vernon Dr. Victory. 2014. I Am Victory Kingdom Principles To A Victorious Life: Victory Media and Publishing Company.

Positive Affirmations

A positive affirmation is whenever we provide emotional support verbally or in writing to someone. It generally is a short sentence or phrases that can be repeated daily to motivate, inspire, and encourage someone for completing a goal. Affirmations are crafted with a lot of thought and each word has a meaning and purpose for those that are hearing and listening to them. They are usually concise and to the point this is what makes them so effective in the morning because they start your day with confidence, hope and energy.

Positive affirmations are extremely important and very powerful for teens because they provide a boost to your moral. Affirmations can be sent via text message, left as a post-it note on the fridge, in a backpack and as a recorded message. I use affirmations everyday to encourage myself. In I Samuel 30:6 (AMPC), "But David encouraged and strengthened himself in the Lord His God" I speak positive affirmations over my life daily. Here are some examples affirmations listed below.

Sample Positive Affirmations to be used daily.

I am smart.

I can do anything that I put my mind to.

I can be anything that I want to be.

Life has endless possibilities.

I believe in myself.

I am strong and can overcome every adversity.

I am a very important person to me and others.

I accept my weaknesses and strengths.

I do not have to be strong all the time.

I am a unique individual.

I have love for myself and others.

I can make a difference in the world.

I forgive others for their flaws.

I will not compare with another person.

I am beautiful the way God made me.

Positive Character Traits

Character traits are words that describes a person's personality which makes them who they are. It can describe a person's behavior or attitude. Character traits can be positive or negative and are adjectives. Here are some character traits listed below.

Positive Character Traits:

- Generosity
- Integrity
- Loyalty
- Patient
- Cooperative
- Honest
- Respectful
- Forgiving
- Optimistic
- Loving
- Kind
- Helpful
- Bold
- Courageous
- Determined
- Ambitious
- Strong
- Sincere

Youtube Videos

Week 3. Video by India Arie

Week 4. The Greatest Love of All by Whitney Houston

Week 5. Champion by Carrie Underwood/Ludacris

Week 6. See You Again by Whiz Khalifa

Week 7. Don't You Worry About A Thing by Tori Kelly

Week 8. Lovely Day by Demi Lovato

Week 9. Roar by Katy Perry

Week 10. No Fear by Kari Jobe

Week 11. Help us to Love by tori Kelly/The Hamiltones

Week 12. Spread Love by Take 6

Week 13. Prayer by Andrea Bocelli/Celine dion

Week 14. Imagine by John lennon

Week 15. Under pressure Mindfulness Meditation for Teens (www.2bpresent.com)